MOSAIC

The work of the Muses

A short survey

by
Gabriella Fiorucci Pascarelli

Dedicated to the sleeping Muse in all of us

Foreword

*The aim of this book is to present a concise and yet clear
introduction to a complex subject such as that of mosaics.
It is not an academic publication, rather it should be
regarded as a first step into a magical world where the
reader is invited to follow and understand the long path of
this millenary art which has in the course of the centuries
produced remarkable masterpieces, many of which we are
luckily still able to admire today.*

*Standing in front of any given mosaic (and indeed there is
such a large variety of them), we cannot but stop and muse
on the beauty and meaning these works want to convey to
us. Design, materials, technical skills, not least patience, all
aimed at the production of works that capture our
imagination and arouse in us admiration and awe.*

*It is certain that there is today a renewed interest in this form
of art as old as man, an art that obviously has evolved
throughout the centuries both in technique, materials and
contents.*

*The most famous personage that we know of and who was
enthralled by the beauty of mosaics was Julius Caesar.
According to the Latin writer Svetonius, even during his war
campaigns, the dictator brought with him mosaic emblemata
(Svetonius, Divus Julius 46).*

*In reading these pages the visitor who having fallen in love
with this art will bring home a mosaic bought in Rome or in
other cities will certainly appreciate more fully the work that
will later adorn his house and in which the artist has literally
infused "piece by piece" his energy, creating or re-creating
new and ancient splendours.*

First Edition January 2000

ISBN 88-900425-0-8

Printed by XPress - Rome

MOSAIC

The work of the Muses

by

Gabriella Fiorucci Pascarelli

A number of individuals and institutions have been of assistance in the course of my research and I am grateful to them all. In addition to those named in the photographic acknowledgements, I should like to thank particulary Mr. Francis (Bob) Nash, B.A. Art and English, for his patient work of revision of the English manuscript, and my friend Silvana Mazzoni for word-processing the manuscript and for letting me publish some of her personal photographs.

My husband Vincenzo has also been very supportive in this endeveaour and of special help in the proof-revising and laying out of the book.

5

2   *FOUR MUSES (Mosaic panel, II cent. A.D.?)*
Only four of the nine Muses, daughters of Jupiter and Mnemosyne.
Each presided over a particular department of art, literature and
science.
MUSEO NAZIONALE ROMANO, ROME

Introduction

In the "Museo Nazionale Romano" in Rome is to be seen a panel showing *four Muses.*
From Greek mythology we understand that they were nine in number and were regarded as the daughters of Zeus and Mnemosine (Memory). Each of them presided over a different branch of the arts and sciences[1].Their cult was linked with that of Apollo. In the Vatican Museums there is a room dedicated to them where besides the statues of the young girls, one can admire *Apollo himself,* the poet-laureate par excellence who advances as he plays his personal musical instrument, the kythara or lyre.
According to mythology, the Muses resided not only in Parnassus but in several other places which were always identified with woods, grottoes, water-springs and the like, that is sites where the inspiration of the poet or the artist was enhanced by the intimate communion with Nature, where the Muses could better work.
We understand that the Latins called mosaic **opus musivum**, literally "the work of the Muses". The origin of mosaic is controversial. Man has always sought to apply materials that will withstand the test of time, and certainly mosaics give a great sense of durability and stability.
Originally it was an art strictly linked to architecture.

2

1

---

[1] The nine Muses are **Melpomene**, presiding over tragedy, **Erato** the muse of love poetry, **Clio** whose domain is history, **Polyhymnia**, patroness of lyrical poetry, **Thalia**, the muse of comedy, **Tersichore** the inspirer of dance, **Urania** ruling over didactic poetry and astronomy, **Euterpe** the muse of music and finally **Calliope** inspiring epic poetry. The latter was regarded as the mother of Orpheus. The muses are also linked with other words such as museo, the very place sacred to them and in later times indicating the walls and vaults decorated in mosaics of the grottoes and fountains of the Roman garden.
Museo indicated also that building in Alexandria of Egypt where scholars and philosophers of the ancient world found hospitality, and Museo was the name of the poet-priest, disciple of Orpheus, recognized as the inventor of the hexameter.

Contents

Classical
and
Medieval
World

4 ORPHEUS PLAYING THE LYRE (III cent. A.D.)
*The Tracian Bard is sorrounded by various animals,
enchanted by the sweet melodies of the kythara*
MUSEUM OF MOSAICS, ANTYOKA, TURKEY

- 1 -

Origin of Mosaic
and the Graeco-Roman World

It is well known that mosaic art was already practised by the Chaldeans as wall decoration. As it can be seen in the *columns of the temples at Uruk*, mosaic tesserae have been embedded in the mud walls both as a decoration and as a way to strengthen the structure. The materials used were fragments of coloured terracotta[2].

From the Chaldeans, the oldest example known to us as a mosaic panel is the so-called *"Royal Standard of Ur"*, today visible in the British Museum, a work dating back as early as year 2500-2600 B.C.

Probably other examples of this kind were made, but only this one survived into modern times. Its real use is uncertain.

5
DEER HUNT
(IV cent. B.C.)
*Pebble mosaic
measuring
cm310x310
PELLA MUSEUM,
PELLA,
MACEDONIA*

The Standard of Ur consists of four mosaic panels of shell and red limestone against a background of lapis lazuli chips embedded in bitumen, originally set in a wooden framework. The trapezoidal panels at each end show animal scenes, but they are indeed very damaged and hardly visible. Happily the two main panels are very well preserved and scholars refer to them as "War" and "Peace" because they seem to illustrate a military victory and the subsequent celebration banquet. Evident in this very old work is the very "modern" technique of semiprecious materials cut in the same manner as the Roman *opus sectile*; and because they are portable they can also be regarded as the most ancient example of *emblemata* (see glossary).

In ancient times the Latin writer Pliny had no doubts about the origin of mosaic floors which he believed to be a Hellenistic invention. According to his own words "pavimenta originem apud Graecos habent" (Pliny, Naturalis Historiae).

6 COLUMNS OF URUK (Babylonian architectural decoration)
Removed from the city of Uruk (modern Warka) in Irak.
STAATLICHES MUSEUM, BERLIN.

7 ROYAL STANDARD OF UR (ca. 2600 B.C.)
*One of the four panels excavated in the Royal Cemetery
at Ur, Irak, measuring cm 22x47, showing a war scene.*
BRITISH MUSEUM, LONDON

Remains of pavements formed with marble chips, white or coloured, set into a very compact and strong mortar have been found in Egypt, Mesopotamia and Greece.

From Pliny and other sources of evidence, it is assumed that the time of introduction of mosaic pavement into Rome was about 80 B.C.

In Rome, fragments of this type of pavement (pavimentum testaceum, that is made of crushed potsherds) have been discovered in the house underneath the Church of St. Peter in Chains (S. Pietro ad Vincula) and also in the Ludus Magnus and under the Tabularium. The former being the most important school for the training of the gladiators connected with the fighting in the Colosseum and the latter the State Archive for the keeping of the tablets of the law and other political documents.

It is certain that mosaic schools existed in Egypt from where its application spread all over the Mediterranean world.

The Egyptians were also very skilled producers of glass, indeed Pliny attributes to them the invention of it, and traces of mosaic decorations with glass material have been found on the inner walls of the temple of Ramses II in Heliopolis. Unfortunately not many mosaic works have

13

come to light in Egypt, but the surviving few are all of very fine quality. In the Egyptian Museum in Turin is on exhibition a 4th century B.C. sarcophagus with the lid "encrusted" with faience pieces, proving that the craft was also applied to objects and not only to architectural features.

8 DIONYSUS RIDING A PANTHER (II cent. B.C.)
Floor Mosaic of the god thought to be the Initiator
to immortality
HOUSE OF THE MASKS, DELOS, GREECE

The Hellenistic culture

The Hellenistic age was a very creative time for the production of mosaics.

From a chronological point of view this age may be taken as starting with the death of Alexander the Great (circa 330 B.C.) and his teacher Aristotle – the intellectual father of the Hellenistic age[3] – and ending with the death of Julius Caesar (Hellenistic-republican period).

The immense territory ruled by Alexander at his death was divided among his generals who founded various dynasties.

In the art field it was a period in which grew the awareness of the great Greek heritage which the old cities wanted to preserve, along with the more "modern" outlook of the new local dynasties.

Great libraries were founded to preserve and edit books and it was also then that art collections were being formed. The art of copying may also be said to have been born then when the great masterpieces were

9   BATTLE OF ISSUS (II/I cent. B.C.)
Mosaic showing the famous battle of Alexander against Darius.
Found at Pompei in the House of the Faun.
MUSEO ARCHEOLOGICO NAZIONALE, NAPLES

being copied to meet the great demand for works of art by private collectors, many of whom lived in Italy.

The sculptors of the time were Lysippos, Praxiteles, Leochares, Briaxis, Skopas and the great painters were Pausia, Euphranor, Nikias and Apelle of Ephesus.

The Hellenistic world offers very good examples of mosaic pavements[4] which were often confined to the men's dining-room where dinner was followed by the symposion.[5] Their designs were very much influenced by the patterns of the textiles that would be hung on the walls.

These early mosaics were first made with pebbles as shown in the splendid examples found at Pella and Olynthos. Pella was the Macedonian capital where Alexander was born, some thirty kilometers west of Salonika.

5   The Pella pebble mosaics were found in two houses of rich patrons. One shows *a deer hunt*, signed by Gnosis and dated by scholars around 320-300 B.C. The central scene is surrounded by a mixed floral border where besides the bunch of acanthus leaves can be recognised roses, crocuses, lilies, and euphorbias. The pebbles used show a considerable colour range and the linear quality of the figures is enhanced by leaden strips that outline some of them.

The other mosaic shows Dionysus and the lion hunt, probably referring to an actual hunt in which Alexander participated when he was saved by his friend Krateros.

At Olynthos (a town south of Thessalonika) the mosaic dated a little earlier (ca. 345 B.C.). It shows Bellephoron on his winged horse Pegasus fighting the Chimera. Compared to the Pella mosaics, here the pebbles are much simpler and coarser. The theme of Bellephoron[6] persisted for many centuries and has been found even in a 4th century A.D. mosaic in Dorset, Britain.

As for pebble mosaics in Italy, the oldest one was found in Sicily at Morgantina, but in this mosaic stone tesserae are also inserted and therefore is regarded as a landmark in the passage from pebble to cut tesserae mosaics.

To the middle Hellenistic period belong the mosaics of the Doves, the *asaraton* floor and the Homeric scenes on Hiero's ship, now lost.

10   *The Doves mosaic* is also known as "Pliny's Doves" as it was this Roman writer who in his "Historia Naturalis" mentions them and Sosos of Pergamon, as the author of the original work, who thereby gained his

16

fame for ever. Sosos is supposed to have gathered around him a famous school at Pergamon. The artists of this circle were much concerned with the rendering of reality in the minutest detail and with illusionistic and trompe-l'oeil effects. This could be obtained by using very small tesserae, in carefully graded shades, the artist having at his disposal a large "palette" of colours.

The Doves are shown drinking water on the edge of a metal vessel and we can admire a fine copy of it in Rome in the Capitoline Museum. There is a suggestion that the mosaic is a light-hearted interpretation of Nestor's cup[7] in the XI book of the Iliad. It was found together with other mosaics now housed in the Vatican, at Hadrian's Villa at Tivoli, near Rome, by cardinal Furetti.

10 PLINY'S DOVES (II cent. A.D.)
Found at Hadrian's Villa at Tivoli. A much copied subject.
MUSEI CAPITOLINI, ROME

This villa was the countryside retreat of the emperor by the Anio river at the foot of the Tiburtini Hills. Since his adolescence Hadrian was imbued with Greek culture, mastering the language which he loved above all those others which he also spoke fairly well having learned them during his long stays abroad. The villa included many halls, porticoes, temples, libraries, etc. all finely decorated with frescos, mosaics, stuccoes worthy of the emperor's refined taste.

12   The mosaics in the Vatican Museum also found at Tivoli, represent pastoral subjects, a fight between a lion and a bull and *masks with attributes of Apollo and Dionysus*, respectively a griffon and a panther. They have been restored by the mosaicists of the Vatican Studio after they were found, ca. 1779. To Sosos of Pergamon is also attributed the invention of
14   the so-called *asaraton floor* (unswept). Numerous specimen survive and a remarkable example of this type can be admired in the Vatican Museum.

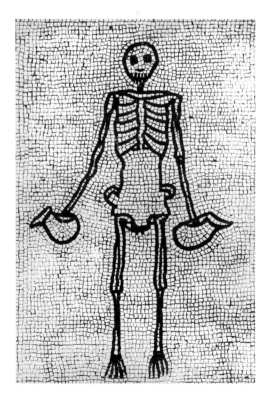

11
SKELETON
(Larva)
HOLDING
A WINE
VESSEL
IN EACH HAND
(I cent. A.D.)
Larva "present"
at a Roman
banquet.
MUSEO
ARCHEOLOGICO
NAZIONALE,
NAPLES

12 MASKS MOSAIC (II cent. A.D.)
*Three of the four emblemata show theatrical masks, whilst the fourth
consist of a pastoral scene. Found at Hadrian's Villa at Tivoli.*
GABINETTO DELLE MASCHERE, MUSEO PIO-CLEMENTINO, VATICAN CITY

The floor shows the remnants of food and clearly comes from a triclinium (dining-room)[8a]. In fact guests customarily threw pieces of discarded food, such as legs of lobsters, shells of snails, cores of apples, etc.
on to the ground. After dinner there was certainly a lot of cleaning up for
the slaves to do!

This habit, which may indeed seem very strange to us, was instead
very common at the dinner tables then and had a symbolical meaning.
According to scholars, the remnants of food represented an offering to

the *larvae (shades)* of the deceased ones who populated the dining rooms. The Roman banquet in fact took place almost like a religious ceremony and was full of acts and behaviours that today most of us would regard as superstitious[8b].

The Homeric scenes from the Iliad on Hiero' ship decorated the floor of the dining room of this enormous ship built around 265-215 B.C. by the tyrant of Syracuse who presented it to Ptolomey IV, also another great lover of Homer. Unfortunately none of these mosaic scenes have survived to-day[9].

Another artist to be remembered is Idoskourides who signed the mosaics from a villa at Pompei, a scene from a Comedy and Women at breakfast, both dating from 100 B.C. These are now in the Museo Nazionale in Naples.

Belonging to the middle Hellenistic period too are the three mosaics with dramatic subjects found in the so called "House of the Masks" at Delos. On this island flourished a lively theatrical life which is reflected in the decoration of the houses excavated in the area.

In the House of the Masks the mosaics were in three adjoining rooms (see *map of the house*)

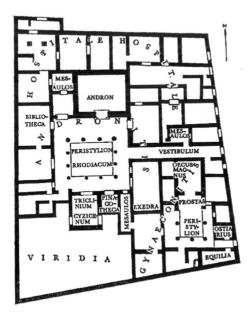

13
PLAN OF THE
GROUND FLOOR
OF THE HOUSE
OF THE MASKS AT
DELOS
(II cent. B.C..)
GREECE

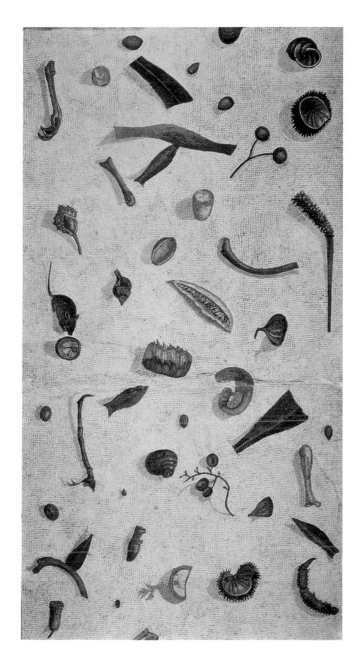

14
ASARATON
(Unswept) FLOOR,
showing remnants
of discarded food
(II cent. A.D.)
*From the Aventine
Hill, Rome.*
*MUSEO
GREGORIANO
PROFANO,
VATICAN CITY*

15
NILOTIC SCENE
(I cent. A.D.)
*Rendered
with great
awareness of the
environment.
From the Temple
of Fortuna
Primigenia
at Praenestre.
MUSEO
ARCHEOLOGICO,
PALESTRINA,
ITALY*

In a room the mosaics are comic masks hanging from a trailer of fruited ivy, including those of Pan and a satyr. This mosaic is in the room called "andron". The other mosaic in a smaller room shows a flute-player and a dancer wearing a bald mask with a wreath around it. The third mosaic in the room on the right of the andron shows *a figure seated on a panther.* It has being identified with young Dionysus. The God rides a panther because his travels took him to India and he was nursed by this animal. He is the god of satyrs and maenads and the initiator to immortality. He is also the god of tragedy and the god of the symposion.

The House of the Masks is situated not too far from the theatre, and the archaeologists who participated in the excavations have been led to believe that the house was connected in someway with the theatre itself, probably the property of a rich patron of drama.

Hellenistic centres in Italy were numerous as the Romans, since times of old, had always been in contact with the Greek world before they conquered it. They were always fascinated by the art of the Greek artists who came to Italy in great number, and here we remind the reader of the famous epigram of Horace "captive Greece conquered its savage captor".

Therefore to Hellenistic centres are ascribed those magnificent Nilotic scenes, like the two famous examples of Pompei and Palestrina, near Rome.

In Palestrina (ancient Praenestre) during the Republican period (1st century B.C.) was built a *Temple to Fortuna Primigenia.* The structure rose on six different levels. On the lower one was found a magnificent mosaic showing in a pictorial way a *Nilotic scene with human figures* (peasants, soldiers, a group at leisure, etc.) *and animals,* above all those living in the delta of the river, such as crocodiles, hippopotamuses, ibisis etc. drawn with a perfection that reveals a keen interest and spirit of observation of the animal kingdom on the part of the "pictor imaginarius".

The mosaic is exceptionally large. In fact it measures 6.15m x 6.06. The scene is shown in a sort of experimental bird's eye view perspective, but with many other elements presented in the normal horizontal way. A mosaic like this was certainly a copy of a painting. As the original paintings are lost, the mosaic copies are for us of an incalculable value to appreciate the skill or the "bravura" of these ancient masters. We understand that at the court of Alexander a large circle of artists was active, among whom Apelle was acclaimed as the most important of the court painters.

16

TEMPLE OF FORTUNA
PRIMIGENIA AT
PRAENESTRE
*Hypothetical recontruction
by arch. L. Canina in the
early 1800.*
PALESTRINA, ITALY

17

CAVE CANEM
*Mosaic in the "black and
white" style found in the
House of the Tragic Poet
at Pompei.*
*MUSEO ARCHEOLOGICO
NAZIONALE, NAPLES*

In the XVII century the mosaicist G.B. Calandra (who was then the head of the Vatican Studio) restored the work whose many parts had been detached from their original place to be transported to Rome. A second "stacco" occurred during the Second World War, as the mosaic was cut into large portions to preserve them in Rome for the duration of the conflict. Today this mosaic is visible in the Museo Nazionale Archeologico Prenestrino at Palestrina.

In classical times we find plenty of geometric designs, which include

18   OCEANUS (II cent. A.D.)
The sea-god Oceanus in seen in the center of a floor mosaic found at Ostia, where the black and white style is seen at its best.
MARITIME BATH, OSTIA (ROME)

19   SKETSCH OF A WATER ORGAN
Taken from a mosaic floor at Nennig (Germany). Nero showed much interest in this instrument and hydraulic organs of new construction were built during his reign.

swastikas, meanders (Greek keys) double and triple braided patterns, laurel wreaths, etc. We will look at them at the end of the book, in "How a mosaic is made".

The Roman World

Responsible for the proliferation of mosaic pavements were the Romans, who spread this art all over the provinces of their empire, so much so that mosaic pavement is considered "ars romana" par excellence and there is no colonised area where traces of mosaics are not found.

Thus it comes as little surprise that in Rome there was not a house which could not boast at least one room paved with mosaics. The "mass production" of the time must have been in many cases the work of simple craftsmen who most probably copied the repertory of others' designs, since not everyone possessed the requisite imagination to produce his own subjects.

In the Roman house, one part of the structure that was certainly covered with mosaic, however simple this might have been, was the impluvium in the inner hall, where the rain water gathered and where the mosaic certainly glinted and freshened its colour when rained upon.

Normally the subjects of the mosaics vary according to the period and place to which they were destined. Sometimes it adapts itself more specifically to a room, such as the already mentioned *asaraton floor* of the triclinium or the brawny *athletes in the palestra* of Caracalla Baths.

14
20

The artist, if he was imaginative enough, could create innumerable compositions of the most varied kind, not only geometric designs, but masks, races in the circus, battle scenes, musical instruments, marine scenes, etc. For this reason, apart from their artistic value, mosaics are an inexhaustible source of information for us to learn about the Romans' habits, either in private daily life or in their public roles.

From a magnificent mosaic in a villa at Zitlen, North Africa, we can see the commencement of gladiatorial games. Before the actual combat started, raucous music was played with trumpets, horns and even a *water-organ*[10].

19

Among the personages mostly represented in Roman mosaics are sea divinities and animals, first of all Neptune and tritons, these subjects being well fitted for the decoration of rooms where a lot of water was used as in the case of the large termae and private baths. A splendid mosaic showing the Triumph of Neptune is in the Bard Museum in Tunis, where the god, with his trident, emerges from the ocean standing in his chariot pulled by sea-horses.

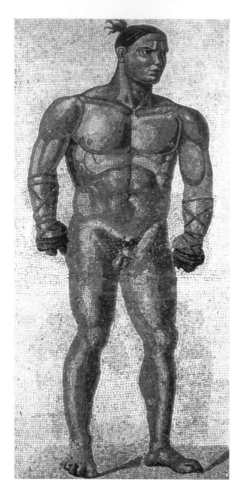

20
PUGILIST
(II cent. A.D.)
The athlete is shown
wearing boxing gloves!
The match went on
without interval until
one of the two
contendents succumbed.
From the Baths of
Caracalla.
MUSEO GREGORIANO
PROFANO,
VATICAN CITY

Another frequently represented god was Dionysus, often portrayed in triumph in his chariot pulled by tigers, or perhaps languidly lying in his boat as this is suddenly attacked by pirates who are promptly repulsed and pushed back into the sea by the boatmen where they are quickly transformed into fish.

However it seems that holding the record for being *the most repre-sented figure is Orpheus*, of whom so far have been listed more than seventy mosaics with his effigy.

Orpheus is the mythical Thracian bard playing and singing so well, accompanied by his lyre, that even wild animals would gather around him in peace to listen to the sweet sounds. His mother was the Muse of

4

Epic poetry, Calliope. Orpheus is said to have introduced sacred rites and religion into Greece as well as astrology and magical arts. His chants were the invocations used in the Eleusinian misteries and so great was his reputation that at a later time he was deified[11]. It must be noted here that in the passage to the Christian iconography the mythical bard was assimilated as the Good Shepherd or as suggested by some scholars as David, he himself a shepherd, poet and musician.

For easy reference scholars tend to distinguish in the Roman world four major phases in the development of mosaic art. Some of course overlap one another, but for simplicity we name them as follows:

1st phase - The republican-hellenistic period: the most famous example is the *"Battle of Issus"* between Alexander the Great and Darius, the Persian Monarch. It can be viewed in the National Archaeological Museum in Naples. All experts agree that it is a copy of an original painting, perhaps by Philoxenos of Eretria (317-315 B.C.)[12]. This, like the already mentioned *mosaic of Palestrina*, reveals a close relation between mosaic and painting, a relation that will always be the guideline for almost every mosaicists in the centuries to come. According to Prof. Gullini these two works were made by the same Alexandrian mosaicists with the use of tiny tesserae to achieve the pictorial effect.

2nd black and white phase, which was prevalent in Italy through all the 1st, 2nd and 3rd centuries. This is also the period of the so-called "watchdog" series, of which the most famous one is the *"Cave Canem"* ("Beware of the dog") at the entrance of the "House of the Tragic Poet" in Pompei. In this dog-series there is often an addition of red colour for the detailing of tongue and leash.

In the black and white mosaics the subjects are depicted in their simplest form, perspective is ignored and the human or animal figures result in two dimension stylised silhouettes rather than in three dimension realistic representation. It has been noted that the effectiveness of the black and white mosaic lies in its ability to convey essentials while preserving its integrity as an art independent from painting. In spite of being more economical they could on the contrary produce effects of surprising power.

3rd phase – The floral style or "stile fiorito" phase that appears early second century under the reign of Hadrian. The "stile fiorito" marks the highest point reached by the black and white mosaics.

Black and white mosaic can be studied at its best at *Ostia*, ancient port of Rome and therefore the one-time commercial capital of all the Mediterranean basin. No less than 450 mosaics have been listed in this town which deserves at least a one day visit. In the Palace near via della Foce, have been discovered both black and white and polychrome mosaics of such fine workmanship contrasting other modest pieces found elsewhere in the town.

Hadrian's reign saw the re-emergence of the polychrome mosaic in Italy and of the so-called "pseudo-emblemata" in the pavements. These have to be regarded as panels made in situ and not in the workshop, and then framed to give the illusion that they were transportable, as were the real emblemata, but in reality they were not movable.

4th and last phase is the polychrome style, such as seen in Sicily at Piazza Armerina in the Imperial Villa of Maximian, father of Maxentius, rival of the first Christian Emperor Constantine.

The villa was probably a hunting lodge, including something like 64 rooms for a total surface of 4500 square meters. Every single room is covered with floor mosaics. The subjects are varied: hunting scenes, the labours of Hercules, the theme of Odysseus in the cave of Polyphemus, wild beasts in the arena, ten *girls engaged in different sports* (wearing very modern bikinis!) and much, much more.

The style of Piazza Armerina seems to combine both the Hellenistic and Italian traditions. The mosaics were most probably executed by African mosaicists imported for the purpose.

Another example of the polychrome style is the one at Aquileia, in the Northern Italian region of Friuli, with the aquatic scenes of the Paleochristian basilica, about year 314. In this case though we are passing to a further development of the mosaic, that is the one appropriated by the Christian world.

At this stage aquatic scenes with fish were growing popular because of the message carried by the fish (ictus in Greek) forming the initials of Iesos Christos Theou Uios Soter (<u>or</u> Jesus Christ Son of God, Saviour), symbol so pregnant of meaning to the Christians. On the side of the Aquileia mosaic there is an inscription that informs us that the work was undertaken with the financial help of the congregation.

In the Provinces

All over the empire flourished the provincial schools. In France, Germany and Spain persisted a severe style and the acceptance to a certain extent of the black and white floral style of Italy.

In Southern France, mosaics were found in Vienne, Arles, Nimes, St. Colombe. The repertory is based on the geometric patterns and besides the black and white designs can be seen pavements completely covered with emblemata linked one another with braided motifs.

The city of Vienne, a few kilometres south of Lyon, occupied a strategic point in Roman times, soon recognised by Julius Caesar. In fact at Vienne crossed two major ways of circulation, namely the valley of the Rhone and the route to the Alps. For this reason the town was granted the privilege of becoming a Latin colony.

In the local Archaeological Museum are preserved various mosaics of

21 SHE-WOLF AND TWINS (I cent. A.D.)
Naif and yet realistic rendering of the Roman myth.
LEEDS MUSEUMS AND GALLERIES, LEEDS, ENGLAND

the area, some of them accidentally found during the building of modern edifices.

The mosaics are both in the "black and white" and polychrome styles.

22

The black and white mosaics are mainly geometric (with the exception of the mosaic of the Ocean Gods) representing four heads of the sea god at the four corners of the composition (only two are entirely preserved): the faces are old men with long hair and beards surrounded by fish and other sea animals. The themes of the polychrome mosaics are the classical ones, including Orpheus playing the lyre, panthers, lions, sea-monsters, etc. Of exceptional beauty and unusual content is by contrast the so-called *Mosaic of Lycurgus* (end of the 2nd century A.D.). Found in the locality of St. Colombe-les-Vienne in 1900 it has undergone restoration and is presented in the centre of the Museum. The scene shows the king of Thracia, Lycurgus, as he is desperately trying to save himself from the ever-growing vine-branches that envelop him, and that in spite of his efforts choke him to death[13]. The rendering of the vine branches and leaves, with the many birds hidden among them is very pictorial and the figure of Lycurgus in the middle that tries to free himself with an axe shows great tension and movement.

Almost the same development can be noticed in Germany where there was really a kind of fascination with geometric designs and square panels.

In Britannia the oldest mosaic found dates back to circa 60-70 A.D. and was discovered in the bath of the II Legion at Isca Dumnorium, that is in the modern city of Exeter in Devon. It consists of a small fragment showing the forelegs of a horse galloping towards the sun.

The invasion of Britain took place under the reign of Claudius in A.D. 43: from that time onwards the mosaics that were laid in different locations were certainly at first the work of imported mosaicists, as seen in the Flavian Palace at Fishbourne laid in the black and white Italian style. The repertory of the mosaics remains normally very classical. By studying the many mosaics found either complete or fragmentary, British specialists speak of about 1500 mosaics in Roman Britain. However many are lost. The design of Roman-British mosaics always include geometric patterns, often very elaborate, even if there are representations of human figures and animals in panels laid not necessarily in the centre but in symmetric position all over the covered area. The design of a number of IV century mosaics appear to imitate the decoration of domes.

22 LYCURGUS (II cent. A.D.)
The King of Thracia crushed to death by vine branches.
MUSEE ARCHEOLOGIQUE DE SAINT ROMAIN EN GAL, VIENNE, FRANCE

We think it nice to see an adaptation of the myth of *Romulus and Remus saved by the she-wolf* in the mosaic that has been discovered at Aldborough, North Yorkshire. According to D.B.Toynbee in his "Art in Britain under the Romans" page 284 "...this picture is almost comic in its naivety". Very rare is instead the mosaic pavement found in the county of Dorset at Hinton St. Mary, but now housed in the British Museum. It depicts *Christ as a young man* with soulful eyes and his own monogram, while at the four corners personages identified as the four evangelists: this mosaic has been dated around the years 335-355 A.D.

The production of mosaics in Northern Africa took a complete different course. Almost no black and white style even if this was not

21

25

unknown, but instead colour everywhere. The polychrome style allowed a very lively and pictorial realism.

In this province are found mosaics dated from the I to the V century and well into the Byzantine period too. An estimate of about 2000 mosaics is not an exaggeration. For the most part mosaics were made for the villas of the dignitaries of the empire built between the desert and the sea. The locations were Zitlen, Sabrata, Leptis Magna, etc. The repertory is very ample, from geometric to vegetable patterns, to human figures, gods and animals.

A very detailed account of the African mosaics can be read in the book "Italy in Africa" Vol. I "The mosaics of Tripolitania" by A.

23 ROMAN GIRLS IN A PALESTRA (IV cent. A.D.)
Girls practising their excercise in a gym attired in bikinis!
SALA DELLE DIECI RAGAZZE, PIAZZA ARMERINA, SICILY

24 HUNTING SCENE (IV cent. A.D.)
Detailed scene of wild-boar hunting, of which the Romans were very glottonous. THE BARDO MUSEUM, TUNIS

Aurigemma. A team of Italian archaeologists in fact led a research in Tripolitania from 1911 to 1943 when Lybia was liberated by the British.

At Sabratha, in Oceanus Bath, are to be seen the famous head of Oceanus himself and the bust of Diana-Luna. In this town were found four Christian basilicas, one of which, the Justinian Basilica, built after the reconquest of Africa at the hand of Justinian's general Belisarius in 533 A.D. This basilica is famous for its floor mosaic that according to the description of G.Guidi "is a mystical representation of the True Vine, bursting with luxuriant vegetation and populated with many different birds, all contributing through the variety of their particular symbolism to

25   BEARDLESS CHRIST (IV cent. A.D.)
*Rare depiction of Christ on a floor. At the four corners personages
identified with the four Evangelists. From Hinton St. Mary, Dorset.
BRITISH MUSEUM, LONDON*

the illumination of the very idea of that Christian life which is to be followed by the eternal joys of Paradise". With this mosaic though we are
already in the ambit of the Byzantine world.

To restrict ourselves here to the "Roman world" must be mentioned
the mosaics of Zliten with its many villas, above all that of Dar Buc
Ammera, amongst the richest in mosaics. Famous are the scenes of gladiators fighting one another (the Retiarus versus the Secutor
Contraretiarius, a Trax versus a Hoplomachus) *venationes scenes*, etc.
plus those showing the punishment inflicted on the leaders of the
Gramantes after their attempt to destroy Leptis Magna. The punishments
consisted in being exposed to a panther while standing on a small
wheeled platform or to the lions in the arena, or forced to separate a bear
and a bull chained together.

Other mosaics show less cruel scenes, such as bucrani and garlands,
baskets with fish, acanthus scrolls and birds, indeed a balanced sympho-
ny of colours and forms.

24

We have already mentioned the importation of African mosaicists for the villa of Piazza Armerina. Their influence was also felt at Centcelles, near Tarragona (Spain) in the first metropolitan church. They produce a combination of secular and religious subjects, namely the four seasons and hunting scenes with two registers of Christian scenes.

In the East, must be remembered the city of Antioch, now belonging to Turkey. It used to be the capital of the Syrian province after the Roman conquest in that part of the world. The role of Antioch has to be considered similar to that of Alexandria in earlier times, that is a centre of great culture. The art in this place was less conservative and the Hellenistic art of the early period came to be soon replaced by the orientalising style of Syria. Some experts see in this style (as seen from fresco paintings in the region) "the oriental forerunner of the Byzantine art".

In Antioch the mosaic floors which are extant are dated between the 3rd and 6th centuries. There was built a special museum to house them but others are found in countries such as France (The Judgement of Paris, at the Louvre) and the U.S.A. (the Drinking contest between Hercules and Dionysus, in the Worcester Museum, Mass). The early mosaics of Antioch can hardly be distinguished from those of North Africa or from the Hellenistic world, while the later ones resemble more the Persian carpets.

NOTES

[2] The Sumerian city of Ur, the Old Testament "Ur of the Chaldees" was excavated by the University of Pennsylvania and the British Museum in the years 1922-1934 under the direction of Sir Leonard Wooley. The variety of materials used by the Mesopotamian craftsmen include gold, silver, shell, lapis lazuli, wood and bitumen.

[3] The ideas of Aristotle affecting art can be succinctly summarised as the establishment of biological categories, of classical ideals and beginning of scholarship

[4] Alexander the Great highly revered the philosopher Dyogenes the cynic. A curious anecdote about this thinker is reported. The cynic, having gone into a private house adorned with a magnificent mosaic pavement showing the Olympian gods, turned around and spat in the owner's face, then he excused himself by saying (in the way of further compliment) that it was the least noble spot he could find in the whole house!

[5] Symposion: (or comissatio of the Romans) second part of a dinner when after having closed the meal by the libation of unmixed wine, the party enjoyed more drinks, listening to music, poetry and having a good time.

[6] Bellerophon was a mythological Greek hero who for a series of circumstances faced several trials, including the killing of the monstrous Chimera. He later tried to ascend Mount Olympus with his winged horse Pegasus, but the Gods resented this attempt and

made him fall from the horse, thus becoming blind and lame. The Chimera was a three-headed monster (lion, goat and serpent) that spat fire.

[7] Nestor: renowned Greek hero that took part together with other bold youths in the expedition by Jason in the search of the Golden Fleece. These youths were called Argonauts from the name of their vessel, Argo, capable of containing fifty men. Nestor, then a youth, bore in his age arms with Achille's and Ajax in the Trojan war. He was by then the oldest of the Grecian chiefs and one to whom they all looked up for counsel. In the IX Book of Iliad, Nestor is the one who advised that an embassy should be sent to Achilles to persuade him to return to the field, when the latter in a dispute with Agamemnon decided to withdraw his forces and openly avowed his intention of returning home to Greece.

[8a] The triclinium was the dining room where the guests were received for the banquets. Normally a square table, but sometimes of round or crescent shape, stood in the centre sorrounded on three sides by three low couches on each side, while the fourth one remained open to the access of the attending slaves. Each couch had room for three people, therefore normally the guests were nine on each side of the central table, nine like the Muses who should have inspired the conversation!

[8b] This strange custom of the Romans though cannot really be discarded too easily, if even today a similar practice is still performed in Zen monasteries in Japan. Basically, before the meal, the monks make a symbolic offering of some rice grains to the invisible hungry spirits dwelling in other spheres and equally any left-over is collected in a special bowl and again distributed to the hungry ghosts. Also the Festival of Feeding the Hungry Ghosts is still part of the yearly celebrations in Zen monasteries all over the world and is observed at the end of the month of October.

[9] Ptolomey IV built a Homereion where a statue of the poet was enthroned. But talking of ships, another famous one, even if of a later period, was that built on the orders of Emperor Caligula for his own amusement. The emperor was notorius for his cruelty. His reign turned into an absolute monarchy, causing his assassination by the hand of a praetorian official. The vessel is now being reconstructed for the amusement of both scholars and tourists.

[10] The invention of the water organ (organum hydraulicum) is ascribed to the Greek Ktesibios. In reality this instrument was well known to the Egyptians too. It was constructed on the syrinx pipe or Pan's pipe and contained 7 pipes made partly of bronze and partly of reed. The sound was produced by waiving the air columns by means of water. It was played on a key-board.

[11] The passion of Orpheus for Eurydice is one of the great love stories of classical myth. When Eurydice died from a snake bite, Orpheus was devasted. After her death Orpheus was so miserable that he visited the realm of the dead to get her back. Even the ferryman Charon, the dog Cerberus and the three judges of the dead were charmed by the sound of his music. The gods of the underworld were so impressed that they allowed Eurydice to be restored to the land of the living. But there was one condition –he should not look back until they were both safely returned. He did not resist and looked back , so he lost her forever. After loosing the beloved for the second time, Orpheus wandered aimlessly. In his desperation he offended Dionysus who set his followers on him and they tore him limb from limb. The Muses found Orpheus's lyre and took it to heaven to form the constellation of Lyra.

[12] Experts are of divided opinion as to the name of the author of the original painting. Besides Philoxenos of Eretria named by Pliny, are also indicated Aristeides of Thebes and Helena, daughter of the Egyptian Timon. The doubt concerning the attribution to Helena is revealed in the question formulated by one of the experts "…but can such a large and powerful picture of a battle scene be the work of a woman?…)

[13] The myth illustrated in the mosaic is the punishment of Lycurgus, king of Thracia. He chased Dionysus who wanted to cross his territories. The king also fell for Ambrosia, Dionysus' nurse. She implored Mother Earth to save her from him. Earth comes to her rescue by opening up and swallowing the girl, quickly transformed into a vine tree. Its branches grew relentlessly and finally enveloped the king's throat so that he died strangled.

26 CALIGULA'S BOAT
Conjectural reconstruction. The ship measured 70m x 20m (230ft x 66ft) and was built of precious wood and decorated with marble and mosaics. It was kept floating on the so called "Diana's Mirror", that is Lake Nemi near Rome.

---

on the following page:

27 CHRIST (IV cent. A.D.)
Standing in the center of the apse on clouds rendered in bold colours. He is flanked (not seen in this picture) by the two brothers Cosmas and Damian, famous healers and patron saints of physicians. CHURCH OF SS. COSMAS AND DAMIAN, ROME

- 2 -

Paleochristian and *Byzantine Mosaics*

With the fall of Rome, it is the paleochristian world that inherits the art by adapting it to the new circumstances, and with Byzantine artists indeed the mosaic art will reach the height of its glory. The large use of glass materials and gold that came to replace the stones of the past, allowed the mosaicists a much richer choice and variety of colours as never to be seen before in the Roman mosaic.

The paleochristian mosaic covers a span of time that goes from the

28 VAULT OF THE MAUSOLEUM OF ST. COSTANZA (IV cent. A.D.)
Detail where classical and pagan motifs are used in this Christian mausoleum, burial of Emperor Constantine's daughters Costanza and Helena. CHURCH OF ST. COSTANZA, ROME

reign of Constantine the Great to about the VII century. It is indeed under the first Christian emperor and the patronage of the Church that the mosaic's possibilities come to be fully realised. From this moment on for almost fifteen centuries mosaic art was at the service of the Church. This is not surprising if we think that the costly art needed surely the sponsorship of wealthy and influential patrons. The two basilicas of St. John Lateran, formerly dedicated to the Saviour and the Old St. Peter's were both built under Constantine and were decorated with mosaics.

The two churches were continually embellished and decorated in

29 ADORATION OF THE MAGI (VIII cent. A.D.)
Mosaic fragment from the rich decoration of the Old St. Peter's Basilica executed under Pope John VII
CHURCH OF ST. MARIA IN COSMEDIN, ROME

30 THE GOOD SHEPHERD (V cent. A.D.)
A nimbed Christ seated on a rock: all the sheep turn their attention to Him.
Compare this mosaic with Orpheus in picture 4.
MAUSOLEO DI GALLA PLACIDIA, RAVENNA, ITALY

later centuries. A *fragment of the Adoration of the Magi* from the old St. 29
Peter's basilica, a work of the VIII century, still survives and is visible in
the sacristy of the church of St.Maria in Cosmedin, while other fragments
are in the Vatican Grottoes and St.Mark's in Florence.

The early IV century is a decisive period of transition and revolution
at the same time. In fact mosaic decorations pass from the pavements to
the walls and vaults, and in doing so new technical solutions had to be
found in order to be able to cover the apses and vaults of the churches.
The new supports (walls and vaults) did not have to be smooth and compact as the mosaics on floors and the use of glass gave more flexibility
and liberty of expression to the artists. The buildings gained an unearth-
ly atmosphere becoming, with mosaic decoration, spiritual and transcen-
dental.

Contents too had by necessity to change. In the transition period we see that typical Roman motifs become christianised. We have already mentioned for example the assimilation of Orpheus as *the Good Shepherd* or as King David. The cupids of the Dionysiac scenes become the cherubs and the peacocks the symbol of immortality of the soul, whilst the acanthus plant is the symbol of the Tree of Life (Arbor-vitae) that supplies the wood of the Cross. A landmark of the transition from classical to paleochristian is visible in the *church of Santa Costanza in Rome,* formerly an imperial mausoleum. According to some scholars there were here even representation, now lost, of panthers, animals sacred to Dionysus. In the middle ages it was referred to as the Temple of Bacchus. In the Basilica of St. Maria Maggiore we see the Roman mosaicists of the V century working on the decoration of the central nave with panels showing scenes from the Old and New Testaments, many of which too damaged unfortunately.

It is important to keep in mind that the decoration of the churches had not only the purpose of embellishing the House of God, but the practical task of teaching biblical stories to people who could neither read nor write. (Also because books were rare!) This aim though is not reached in St. Mary Major as the panels along the central nave are placed to high above and they are too small to be really appreciated by the old or modern visitor.

This is the period when mosaic floors, as known in the Roman world, lose their importance. This must be explained with the obvious decision that no one wanted religious symbols or scenes on the floor where people had to walk. The Christ of Hinton St. Mary, Dorset is indeed a rarity and we know that in A.D. 427 the Codex Theodosianus clearly forbade the use of sacred symbols on the pavements[14]. However there will be a revival of floor mosaics in the Romanesque art (in Otranto, Italy, and in Ganagabie, France), both of the XII century.

Of the same V century, besides St.Mary Major, are extant in Milano the apse mosaics of the Church of St.Aquilino, that show already an Eastern influence as in the Baptistry of St.Giovanni in Naples.

Doubtless the richest and most beautiful mosaics of the Paleochristian world are those to be admired in Ravenna, the city that in the V century was chosen by emperor Honorius as the capital of the Western empire, due to its strategic position near the sea and yet difficult to attack because of the surrounding swamps.

It must be noted that from the exterior most of the edifices of

Ravenna appear very austere and built with simple short bricks with no sign of decoration. On the contrary, inside they display a breathtaking wealth of decoration which is quite unexpected.

Already in the V century magnificent mosaics had been executed in this city in the mausoleum of Galla Placidia, sister of Honorius, who for a time became Regent of the empire on behalf of her son Valentinian.

These mosaics are extremely well preserved to this day. Originally the mausoleum was most probably a shrine dedicated to *the protomartyr St.Lawrence*. In fact inside, in the lunette opposite to the entrance, there is a figure identified with the Roman deacon who was martyred by being burnt on the gridiron.

31

31 ST. LAWRENCE (V cent. A.D.)
The proto-martyr is on the way to his martyrdom, carrying his "own cross".
From a lunette opposite the entrance.
MAUSOLEO DI GALLA PLACIDIA, RAVENNA, ITALY

32 SS. PETER AND PAUL (V cent. A.D.)
The two Apostles fully Roman in their togas are looking up
towards Heaven. At their feet two white doves drink water from a vessel,
symbol of the font of life.
MAUSOLEO DI GALLA PLACIDIA, RAVENNA, ITALY

By studying in detail the other compositions in the edifice, one cannot but notice the perfect adaptation of the decoration to the architecture. Notable are the *images of the two Apostles*, Peter – a strong man with curly short hair and beard – and Paul, as a rather bald man with long hair and beard trimmed to a point. This iconography was already well established and will be handed down throughout the centuries. From this moment on, no one has any doubt on entering any church on who is Peter and who is Paul.

The beauty and the technique of the execution of the mosaics of Galla Placidia reveal the presence of workshops of high artistic standard entirely Roman in both colour and overall composition. *The background in deep blue*, which is characteristic of the early Christian mosaic, again reveals the hand of a fully Roman school. You can see another splendid exemple of

32

27

this on the vault mosaic of the St. Zeno's Chapel in St. Prassede, Rome.

Between the end of the V and the beginning of the VI centuries the mosaic production of the city of Ravenna was under the patronage of the Ostrogoth king Theodoric – himself brought up – as a hostage – at Costantinople and therefore imbued with Eastern Roman culture. He was responsible for the decoration of the Arian Baptistery and the Church of St. Apollinare Nuovo. Both these works present gold backgrounds which became the standard feature of most medieval mosaics. In the old days, St. Apollinare Nuovo was referred to as "the church with the golden sky".

Besides the Arian, there is in Ravenna another baptistery called "The Orthodox Baptistery" or the Neonian Baptistery from the bishop Neon who cared for the interior decoration in the middle of the V century. The dome is appropriately decorated with the Baptism of Christ in the round

33 EMPRESS THEODORA AND HER RETINUE (VI cent. A.D.)
Theodora is carrying an offering for the Holy Mass, a golden chalice for the wine. The lower part of her gown shows the offering of the three Magi.
CHURCH OF ST. VITALE, RAVENNA, ITALY

central panel, while in the outer circular band the twelve apostles stand, one close to the other, each figure separated from the next by an acanthus bush that extends its branches way up.

During the reign of Emperor Justinian, who attempted to regain supremacy for his Eastern Empire over all Italy and the West, was decorated the Church of San Vitale (VI century), in front of whose splendour so many noble spirits, from Dante to Byron, have bowed their heads in reverence[15].

The mosaics of the church, amongst others, display the famous portraits of *Emperor Justinian himself and his wife Theodora*, both followed by their retinue, everyone attired in magnificent regal gowns. The two corteges are placed in the sanctuary area and seem to participate in the sacred mystery for eternity.

In spite of their presence in the mosaics, in reality the imperial majesties never set foot in Ravenna. Their commander-in-chief was General Belisario, that starting from the South of Italy managed to capture Ravenna.

San Vitale is an example of the combination of two different artistic influences, though they seem to be approximately contemporary. One is the Roman influence, with the personages dressed in white, with the backgrounds in blue colour and a rich decoration of acanthus leaves, flowers, fruits, birds, etc. that bestow a very naturalistic and lively atmosphere. The other is the influence of the Byzantine style, as seen in the above mentioned processions of the royal retinues, where the backgrounds are gold, and every figure appears solemn and sacred, belonging to a courtly, sumptuous and hieratic world.

In this brief outline, it is not possible to touch on other Ravenna mosaics, but we like to mention what an unknown poet of the time of Theodoric exclaimed at the sight of these mosaics "Aut lux hic nata est, aut capta hic libera regnat" (Either light was born here, or imprisoned here it reigns free).

Byzantium

By 330 A.D. emperor Constantine had transferred the capital of the empire to Byzantium. Thanks to his victory over Licinio he could re-unify the empire and decided to give it a new capital which was inaugurated on May 11, 330 with the name of "Constantinople".

The transfer to the East was mainly decided to better control the frontiers of the empire on the Danube and the Euphrates, threatened by the

34 ANNUNCIATION (VI cent. A.D.)
Fragment of the semidome with the Archangel Gabriel and Mary.
CHURCH OF ANNUNCIATION, DAFNI, GREECE

Goths and the Persians respectively.

Constantine found a site consisting of an extended area of an older Greek town which had been rebuilt and fortified by Septimius Severus. Its famous hippodrome with its almost 500 meters of length, supplied not only a place of entertainment but also became a centre for the imperial ceremonial. Nearby Constantine built his famous Palace. In planning the new capital, the imitation of Imperial Rome was evident. However the Churches built by Constantine were few, namely St.Irene and the Church of the Apostles where later the Emperor and his successors were buried. The church, now lost, was model for St. Mark's in Venice.

The churches were embellished with mosaics throughout the millennium of Byzantine rule, not only in Constantinople but in all the areas that fell under the dominion of the "Second Rome". Here it must be remembered that the term "Byzantine Empire" is only a convention of modern historians. In fact the inhabitants of this empire called themselves

"Romans" and to them the founder of their empire was certainly Augustus.

From the very start, both Constantine and his successors protected mosaicists with a special law that exempted them from paying any taxes. In this part of the world unfortunately, some damages and replacements occurred during the two iconoclastic periods[16], but apart from this temporary "suspension" mosaics flourished everywhere until the XIV century.

34   Byzantine mosaic is above all wall mosaic and makes use of gold backgrounds, as opposed to the white ones of the classical art. The golden backgrounds normally give the effect of making the figures stand away from the background.

A V century mosaic is the one that covers the cupola of the church of Haghios Gheorghious (St.George's) in Salonika. Remains of VI century
35   mosaics are to be seen in the *Haghia Sophia in Istanbul*, which was built under the reign of Justinian (532-537). Not only the mosaics, but indeed the all structure of the church is a masterpiece of architecture. The historian of the time of Justinian, Procopius writes thus about St. Sophia "… it doesn't seem to have any solid support. Rather it hangs from the sky as if attached to a golden chain and seems to hover in the air".

After the iconoclastic period further decoration was undertaken in the church by different Byzantine emperors, as well as in many other edifices of the city. In Constantinople, the Great Palace of the Emperors was of course decorated with mosaics, though there was more a continuation of the classical style which produced always the effect of a richly patterned carpet.

Byzantine Influence outside Byzantium

The fame of Byzantium and its artists spread widely thanks to pilgrims and crusaders, and it is well documented that Byzantine artists were called to embellish the churches of far distant provinces such as the
37   Ukraine. In Kiev in fact, in the Church of St. Sophia, the *first Byzantine church in Russia* considered to be the model in the following centuries for many other Russian churches, worked Byzantine artists with the help of local artisans who above all ensured the supply of glass which apparently was produced locally. (Excavations on the site have produced evidence of a colour range of at least 170 tints).

This church contains not only mosaics but also frescos. In 1934 more than 3000 square meters of those mosaics and frescos, dating back to the eleventh century were brought back to light. Some details show scenes of

35 MADONNA AND CHILD (XII cent.)
Byzantine mosaic at the entrance of St. Sophia
CHURCH OF HAGHIA SOFIA, ISTANBUL, TURKEY

36/37 TWO "ORANS" (in prayer) FIGURES
One from CEFALÙ, SICILY, and the other from KIEV, UKRAINE

38 SOLDIERS OF THE FOURTH CRUSADE (ca. 1213)
*Detail of the floor mosaic showing in a sort of "pointillisme" style
crusaders ready to launch their spears.*
CHURCH OF S. GIOVANNI EVANGELISTA, RAVENNA, ITALY

courtly life and depict the members of the family of the great Prince
Yaroslav the Wise who built the church (in a famous picture he is shown
offering Christ the model of the same) and whose memory is commemo-
rated in the city which bears his name to this day.

The Byzantine influence in Italy is felt in Sicily for the churches of
Cefalù and Monreale, and in Palermo for the Palatine Chapel. In this city

36

39 DOME OF THE
ROCK (VII cent.)
External view
JERUSALEM, ISRAEL

40 GREAT MOSQUE AT
DAMASCUS (X cent.)
Byzantine work in a
Islamic contest.
Floral and intricate
geometric designs.
DAMASCUS, SYRIA

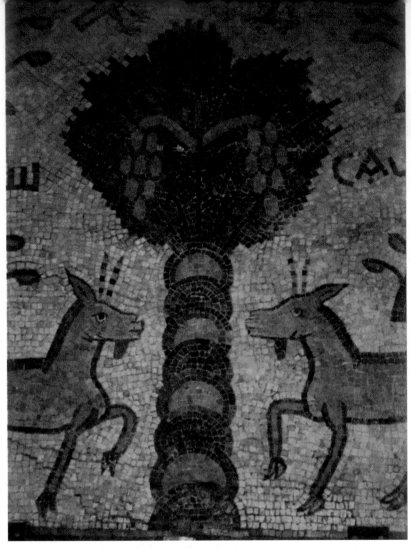

41 PALM TREE WITH TWO DEERS (VI cent. A.D.)
Beatiful symbolic design.
MADEBA, JORDAN

are to be noted in the XII century two profane mosaics, that is the Room of King Roger at the Royal Palace, and the Villa of La Zisa. This is when Sicily was conquered by the Normans and these rulers from the North wanted no doubt to compete with the splendours of the Byzantine capital.

The mosaics of Venice, in St. Marks and in the Churches of the Isles

42 FLOOR MOSAIC OF THE HOLY LAND (VI cent. A.D.)
Oldest representation of Jerusalem
MADEBA, JORDAN

of Torcello and Murano will be touched upon later. They have all been the theme of a wide literature. Other centres were Grottaferrata and Montecassino. Byzantine workers worked for all religions, and their decorations are seen even in far off places as the *Cordova Mosque in Spain* *44* and in the Dome of the Rock in Jerusalem (VII century).

The *Dome of the Rock* is a sacred place of both Muslims and Jews, as *39* the former believe that it is built on the spot where Mohammed made his mystic flight to heaven, and the latter regard the rock as the improvised altar on which Abraham was commanded to sacrifice his son Isaac, as well as the site of the Holy of the Holies in the Jewish Temple. The abstract and geometrical designs from the classical canon allowed the followers of both religions to enjoy mosaic decoration without violating the religious law forbidding the images of animate creatures in their places of worship.

43
PEACOCK
(VI cent.)
*Symbol
of immortality
MADEBA,
JORDAN*

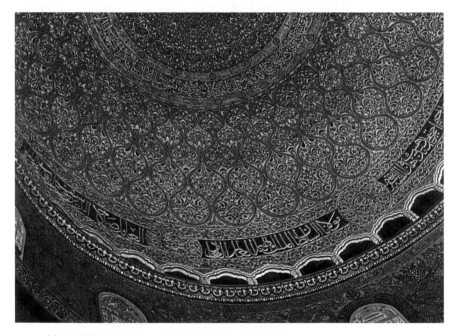

44 INNER CUPOLA OF CORDOVA MOSQUE
*Another example of an Islamic masterpiece executed by Byzantine artisans.
CORDOVA, SPAIN*

Even the *Great Mosque in Damascus*, Syria "the most beautiful thing   *40*
that Muslims own today" (according to what a Muslim writer wrote in
985) was decorated by Byzantine artists.

To remain in the East, some marvelous mosaics can be seen at   *41, 43*
Madeba, Jordan, south-east of the Dead Sea. Here a remarkable "docu-
ment" was found in 1897. It is an unusual *mosaic map of the Holy Land,*   *42*
with a special panel *depicting Jerusalem* where the city is shown with the
mention of all her churches and monasteries. It is said to be the oldest representation of Jerusalem, dating back to about the end of the VI century.

The Romanesque Pavements

Mosaic was an elaborate work to execute, requiring specialized team
work, time and money. During the Romanesque period it needed to be
commissioned by rich patrons, almost always an ecclesiastic of high rank.
Most often, due to the high cost, the floor of the cathedrals were only decorated around the main altar. However in Southern Italy, in the Puglia
region, is to be admired a splendid "carpet-floor" in the Cathedral of
Otranto that in the IX century was seat of a Byzantine government.

The floor mosaics dates from the XII century. It occupies the space of
the entire nave, depicting a tree with many branches, animals and human
figures among them (the tree of Good and Evil, as indicates the presence
of Adam and Eve) and then continues towards the presbytery, apse and lateral aisles with scenes from biblical stories, and pseudo-historical scenes,
such as that of *Alexander ascending to heaven* on his throne drawn by grif-   *45*
fons and scenes from the life of the *"Once and Future King" Arthur.*   *47*

Other Romanesque mosaic floors were made at Brindisi and Ravenna
in the Church of St. John the Evangelist, where the surviving fragments,
following an air raid in 1944, show episodes from *the fourth crusade*, a   *38*
medieval bestiary and even *the mock funeral of a fox.*   *46*

This episode refers to the famous "Roman de Renart" or Reynard the
Fox so very popular in medieval literature and art. All of these mosaics
are rendered in a very simple manner, in a sort of graphic style, with just
a few notes of colour in the bestiary.

At Ganagobie (Alpes de Haute Provence, France) a medieval masterpiece is the floor of the Cathedral which shows a fantastic bestiary and
the combat of armed knights against monsters and chimeras. This floor is
signed by a mosaicist called Trubert.

Many other medieval pavements are found in Romanesque cathedrals and this revival is attributed to Desiderio da Montecassino[17].

45
ALEXANDER
THE GREAT
ASCENDING
TO HEAVEN
(XII cent.)
Detail
of the floor mosaic
CATHEDRAL
OF OTRANTO,
PUGLIA, ITALY

46
REYNART THE FOX
(XII cent.)
Detail of floor mosaic
with the mock funeral
of the fox
CHURCH OF S.
GIOVANNI
EVANGELISTA,
RAVENNA

47 KING ARTHUR (VI cent.)
Detail of the floor mosaic showing a scene of the Arthurian cycle
CATHEDRAL OF OTRANTO, PUGLIA, ITALY

The "Portable Mosaics"

In the ambit of Byzantine mosaic must also be mentioned the artistic expression of the "portable or miniature mosaics" whose subjects are invariably sacred images. They were icons held in great esteem due to their beauty and value because of the difficult technique of using very minute tesserae.

Unlike the icons painted on wood, it seems that mosaic icons were not covered either by silver or gold leaf. It is assumed that they were begun around the XI century and flourished during the period of the dynasty of the Paleologues[18]. These portable mosaics are very rare and were surely well protected being luxury objects for the private devotion for wealthy patrons. Examples of this type of production can be seen in Florence in the Bargello Museum and in the Museum of the Opera del Duomo.

The one in the Bargello is a life-size image of Christ and the other two in the Duomo represent scenes of the Nativity and other salient moments of the life of Jesus, known as *"Byzantine Calendar"*. Another fine mosaic icon of the XIII century is the one showing "the 40 Martyrs of Sebaste" part of the Dumbarton Oak Collection in Washington D.C. and an Annunciation scene housed in the Victoria and Albert Museum in London. Other examples are scattered in the Eastern monasteries.

Such was the devotion of the Medieval Christians that a small mosaic icon depicting the Dead Christ in the sarcophagus aroused great admiration, giving credence to the belief that it had been executed by St. Gregory with fragments of the bones of the martyrs!

The significance of the image (icon) for the Byzantines was different from the significance it bore in the West. The icons were regarded as the testimonies of the presence of the Divine and also as the intermediaries between the world of men and the celestial world. Some of these images were reputed "not made by human hand" (acheiropoietos). Some regarded them as idolatrous, others thought they were legitimate, above all as Christ himself had assumed a human form.

NOTES

[14] Theodosius was also the emperor that established orthodox Christianity as the sole state religion. He carried Constantine religious policy to the extreme conclusion by prohibiting all forms of pagan worship.

[15] Dante, banned from Florence, lived in exile and finally found refuge in Ravenna where he composed a great deal of the third part of his Divine Comedy (The Paradise). He died in this city and the funeral took place in September 1321 in the church of San Francesco. He rests in a tomb by the Franciscan convent.

[16] Iconoclasticism was a religious reformation that occurred in the Byzantine Empire. The followers of the movement were against the use and cult of sacred images, which were thought to be idolatrous and were thus removed from various sites. This occurred during the years 726-87 and 815-43.

[17] Desiderio, abbott of Montecassino, contributef firmly to the establishment of art not only as merely decorative but also as "catechistic" or educational. Great patron of the arts, he was elected Pope with the name Vittore III.

[18] Byzantine Art is defined by various dynasties because art was really bound up with them and their rulers. They are classified and "Justinianic", "Macedonian", "Comnenian" and "Paleologian". The span of time is one millennium from IV century to 1457, the year of the fall of Constantinople to the Turks. The Macedonian art (IX-X cent.) is probably the most important (critics speak of a "Macedonian Renaissance") and lasted about 180 years. The artistic activity, not only limited to mosaic making, was centred around the Great Palace at Constantinople, and the workers were organised in highly exclusive guilds or corporations.

48 SIX OF THE TWELVE FESTIVALS OF THE CHURCH (Early XIV cent.)
Miniature mosaic. Tesserae set on a wax base.
OPERA DEL DUOMO, FLORENCE

The
Renaissance
and the
Modern
World

51
NIMBED ANGEL
(XIII cent.)
*Fragment of the rich
decoration of the Old St.
Peter's Basilica.
Attributed to Giotto
GROTTE VATICANE, ST.
PETER'S BASILICA,
VATICAN CITY*

52 CHRIST ENTHRONED (XIII cent.)
*The Lord is flanked by the Virgin and John the Evangelist.
The only documented mosaic work of Cimabue. Apse mosaic.
THE DUOMO OF PISA, ITALY*

- 3 -

Giotto, Cavallini and Turriti

Back to the West again.

The names of mosaicists are usually not known save in rare cases, but in the medieval period names of artists are being recorded and therefore we know that two great mosaicists appear to be both very active in Rome between the XIII and XIV centuries. They are Pietro Cavallini and Jacopo Turriti, possibly both disciples of Cimabue. To them must be added the name of Giotto. But let us proceed in order.

Cimabue[1] Byzantine is the Florentine master (1240-1302?) considered the founder of the Florentine school. He gave a touch of vigour, realism and drama to the painting of his time. We may say that with him the pictorial art had resurrection after the thraldom of the Byzantine tradition. Well documented as his work is *the superb Christ* and the classical figure of St. John in the apse of the Cathedral of Pisa.

Pietro Cavallini, whose full name was Pietro detto Cavallini dei Cerroni, was both painter and mosaicist. He is considered the founder of the Roman school and certainly drew his inspiration from the paintings of classical and early Christian Rome. Information on his life has been given to us by Giorgio Vasari in his "Lives of famous artists etc." where he accredits him as the disciple of Giotto and having worked with him "in mosaic" in the nave of the old St. Peter's. He was a man of great talent and also able to sculpt. To him is ascribed the famous Crucifix in St. Paul-outside-the wall that, according to tradition, spoke to Saint Brigitte when she came to Rome on pilgrimage. Cavallini died at the ripe old age of 85, working actively till the end.

According to G. Matthiae in his "Medieval Mosaics in the Roman Churches" "... although Cavallini's work is of very high quality he does not use mosaic with the understanding of its special possibilities. He uses it as if it were fresco painting". Indeed Cavallini was an outstanding painter and some of his frescoes can still be seen in Rome.

His mosaic works include the panel of the *"Adoration of the Magi"* to be seen in the Church of St. Maria in Trastevere, Rome and the semi-dome of the same church. These were the works executed for the powerful Stefaneschi family.

52

53

53 ADORATION OF THE MAGI (XIII cent.)
*Notice how the Infant Jesus is ready to receive the gifts and Joseph stands aside
PIETRO CAVALLINI, CHURCH OF ST. MARIA IN TRASTEVERE, ROME*

As Vasari informs us, most probably Cavallini was in contact with
Giotto. This is perhaps the nickname of Ambrogiotto or Ruggerotto or
Parigiotto. A legendary tradition sees in the handsome profile of a youth
wearing a white berret in the frescoes of the Cappella degli Scrovegni at
Padua, the self-portrait of this formidable painter. He is regarded as a
"revolutionary" for he broke up with the rather crystallised Byzantine tradition, in favour of a full freedom of inspiration. Giotto too lived to a ripe
age of 70[2]. He travelled a lot: we find him in Assisi, Padua, Naples, Rome.
Here his presence is well documented towards the end of the XIII centu-

ry, in charge of the frescoes of the Loggia delle Benedizioni in the Lateran Palace on occasion of the first Jubilee year proclaimed by Pope Boniface VIII. The famous mosaic of the Navicella over the entrance of St. Peter's Basilica is attributed to him and is regarded as the conclusion of the Golden Age of the Roman mosaics. "The Navicella" was moved to a number of different places in the past and underwent so many restoration that nothing remains of Giotto's work whatsoever (One of the restorer of the XVI century was Luigi Pace). Probably part of the same "Navicella" mosaics were the famous *angels of the Grotte Vaticane* and of Boville (in the Church of St. Pietro Hispano) not clearly known if by Giotto himself or by some fine artists of his circle.

51

Jacopo Turriti is the author of the apsidal mosaics of the Cathedral of Rome, St. John Lateran, which unfortunately were re-made around the end of the XIX century during the pontificate of Pope Leo XIII, who is buried in the church following his own desire. His skilled art (Turriti was a Franciscan monk) is far better appreciated in the apse of the Basilica of Santa Maria Maggiore, the beauty of which we can still admire in his breathtaking work. In this mosaic there are probably elements of its antique predecessor.

Visitors to Rome always have the opportunity of seeing these mosaics because a visit to the two basilicas is quite often included in tourist itineraries. St. Mary Major is the Marian church par excellence. In the apse we view the *coronation of the Virgin by her Son* while an array of kneeling angels with their delicately tinted wings assist the scene, taking place in a medieval heaven, with fixed stars and the sun and the moon in opposition. This scene anticipates what will be officially confirmed by the Church seven hundred years later. In fact the doctrine of the Assumption of Mary has always been central to the teaching of the Church, and it became dogma only in 1950 under the pontiff Pius XII with a great ceremony held in St. Peter's Square in the presence of more than 100.000 people.

54

NOTES

[1] Not many details of his life are known, but he his supposed to have been of quite strong character, a proud man, a bit arrogant and assuming, the head of a bottega in which was forged a pupil that surpassed him, Giotto, a man of greater genius and a gentler soul. To put it the Florentine way "Ora ha Giotto il grido" (Now Giotto has the fame).
[2] Giotto was a very shrewd person. His life is full of anectodes. When in Naples, King Robert visited him at his work on a very hot summer day. "If I were you" said the condescending King "I would not work when the weather was so hot" "Neither would I" replied promptly the painter looking up at the King with a twinkle in his eyes "if I were you".

54
THE
CORONATION
OF THE VIRGIN
(XIII cent.)
Apse mosaic.
Splendid example
of the skill of the
"Roman School".
JACOPO TURRITI,
BASILICA
ST. MARIA
MAGGIORE,
ROME

- 4 -

Mosaic during the Renaissance

Outside Rome in the XIV century was evolved the decoration of the facade of the Duomo of Orvieto (1310) which a few decades later will find an equivalent in the mosaics of the facade of the *Cathedral of St. Vito in Prague*, following the will of Emperor Charles IV[3]. A link between Orvieto and Prague was already well established for reasons other than artistic. In fact the erection of the Duomo of Orvieto was ordered after a Bohemian priest on his way to Rome, at Bolsena near Orvieto, witnessed the miracle of the "Bleeding Host".

This "Miracle of Bolsena" upon which the Church has based the feast of the Corpus Domini, was immortalised by Raphael in his famous fresco in the Stanze in the Vatican Museum.

55   GOD, THE ETERNAL FATHER (XVI cent.)
Cartoon provided by Raphael
CAPPELLA CHIGI, CHURCH OF ST. MARIA DEL POPOLO, ROME

The cities of Florence and Venice offer a myriad of mosaic works which it is impossible to describe in full in this short essay. It is important to remember that between these two cities there were exchanges of artists, and when a number of Venetian masters died during a pestilence, several Florentine mosaicists were called to go to Venice to replace them.

The "Lagoon City" soon developed strict relations with Byzantium when in the XI century the already powerful Venetian fleet was called to help the capital of the Empire against the threat of the Norman invasion.

This gained Venice several commercial privileges and the Venetian traders soon occupied and lived in the best quarters of Constantinople. Not after long, Byzantine artistic influence was felt in Venice. The most important mosaic works are in the Cathedral of St. Mark which was modelled after the Constantinian Church of the Apostles at Constantinople (now lost).

The mosaics cover all the walls and cupolas of the basilica for an amazing estimated surface of about 4000 square meters. Their executions spans between the XI and XIV centuries, with numerous restorations and alterations of later centuries up to 1800. The materials used were smalti in a large range of colours. The mother city of Venice was Aquileia, whose inhabitants found escape on the laguna islands when threatened by Attila's invasions. Through this Roman town and port "the secret" of the blown glass was passed to the Venetian masters.

To avoid possible fires and accidents the glass factories were established on the island of Murano. A close study of the Marcian mosaics will reveal different periods, techniques and understanding of the possibilities of mosaic art: from Romanesque to Gothic fleurissant, from the purest Byzantine to the novelties of the Renaissance manner.

The subjects are both sacred and historical: scenes from the Old and New Testaments, Prophets and Apostles, Lives of St. Mark and St. Peter. To *the Madonna* is dedicated one chapel called *"dei Mascoli"* where as providers of the cartoons worked amongst others the great Jacopo Bellini, Andrea del Castagno and Andrea Mantegna. The mosaicist was Michele Giambono.

In this chapel for the first time was adopted the technique of the "spolvero" (pouncing) to design the subject on the wall surface, as opposed to the formerly used technique of the "sinopia" drawn with the brush on the mortar where later the tesserae were to be applied.

The arrival in Venice of Florentine artists like Paolo Uccello and others caused the speeding up of the division of tasks between the "design-

57

56 THE ANNUNCIATION (XV cent.)
Lunette of the Door of the Mandorla
DOMENICO GHIRLANDAIO,
CHURCH OF ST. MARIA DEL FIORE, FLORENCE

er" or provider of cartoons (the classical pictor imaginarius) and the actual mosaic-maker: this led soon to the subsequent decadence of the
ancient mosaic tradition of Venice.

58 In Florence is not to be missed the Baptistry opposite the Cathedral
with its *scene of the Last Judgement* that Dante must have studied in
detail![4] The prototype for all other Judgements produced in the course of
the XIV century is the one of the island of Torcello, near Venice, dating
back to the XII century.

The dome of the Florentine Baptistry is the work of the Greek
Apollodorus with the help of the Florentine pupil Andrea Tafi, if we are
to believe the information passed on to us by G. Vasari. Other critics
instead speak of Cimabue and his school, including the Franciscan
Jacopo Turriti whom we have seen very active in Rome.

Another jewel, also from an architectural point of view, is the *Church*

57 DORMITION OF THE VERGIN (XV cent.)
Tuscan and venician masters co-worked in this chapel. Cartoon provided by A. Mantegna.
CAPPELLA DEI MASCOLI, BASILICA OF ST. MARK'S, VENICE

of S. Miniato al Monte (S. Miniato, King of Armenia), where the apsidal 59
mosaics reveal both an influence from Greece and Byzantium.

In the period leading from the end of 1300 to 1800, mosaic art becomes a technique at the service of painting. These are indeed the centuries when mosaic is defined as "pittura di pietra" or "pittura per l'eternità" that is "stone painting" or "painting for eternity". This expression was used by Giorgio Vasari in his book "Lives of the most excellent painters, sculptors and architects", when he quotes the painter Ghirlandaio as saying "the real picture for eternity is mosaic".

Of Ghirlandaio there is a Madonna flanked by two angels in the Cluny Museum, Paris and *the Annunciation* of 1490 in the lunette of the 56
Door of the Mandorla in Santa Maria del Fiore. The two Ghirlandaio Brothers, Domenico and David, were taught the art by Alessio Boldovinetti (1425-1499).

During the Renaissance mosaics were still produced, but artists began to make much more use of the fresco technique for their paintings. This was doubtless a cheaper work to produce! Famous artists such as Paolo Uccello, Andrea del Castagno, Ghirlandaio and others produced in this period mosaics, or drew cartoons for other mosaicists. Not only Vasari dedicated an entire chapter in his "Vite" to the technique of mosaic, but also the well known painter Alessio Baldovinetti wrote a book on the subject of mosaic and its technique. He worked mainly as a restorer of mosaics, without producing original pieces. However, according to Alvar Gonzales-Palacio, in his "Mosaics and Pietre Dure", Baldovinetti carried on for the Florence Baptistery the first "modern" mosaics which we know of. So we see that the tradition is not completely lost and no doubt there existed in Florence in that period a great interest in the mosaic art, and in that of the pietre dure, an interest fuelled by the collecting passion of the Medici.

As for Rome, there are in the Eternal City two major Renaissance works, namely *the Cappella Chigi* in Santa Maria del Popolo whose cartoons for the dome were supplied to the mosaicist Luigi Pace by Raphael and also the underground *chapel of Santa Helena* in the Basilica of

55

61

58
THE INFERNO
(XIII cent.)
*Scenes that must have
inspired Dante!*
*BAPTISTRY,
FLORENCE*

59 BLESSING CHRIST (XIII cent.)
Semidome of the Church of S. Miniato. FLORENCE

60
DETAIL
OF THE
FACADE
OF ST. VITUS
*Most certainly
executed with the
help of Italian
master mosaicists.*
*CATHEDRAL
OF ST. VITUS,
PRAGUE*

S. Croce in Jerusalem, after the cartoon of Melozzo or most probably Baldassarre Peruzzi. This mosaic has been much restored.

In this period we see that due to the high cost of mosaic production, mosaics are painted on the ceilings as in the case of the Stanza della Segnatura in the Vatican!

Mosaic as "pittura per l'eternità" finds its apogee in the decoration of the Basilica of St. Peters in the Vatican, but to this immense work will be dedicated a complete paragraph together with that of the "mosaico minuto"

61 CHRIST AND THE FOUR EVANGELISTS (XVI cent.)
One of the last works of the Renaissance mosaic art. Recently much restored.
CHAPEL OF ST. HELEN,
CHURCH OF ST. CROCE IN GERUSALEMME, ROME

NOTES

[3] During the reign of Emperor Charles IV, the kingdom of Bohemia enjoyed its maximum splendour. The Emperor founded the University of Prague in 1348 (the first in Central Europe) and at his court were received great men of letters and humanists such as Petrarca and Cola di Rienzo.

[4] Dante used to sit inside the Baptistry and call it "il mio bel S. Giovanni". When banned from Florence, the Cathedral and the Campanile by Giotto had not yet been built.

- 5 -

Mosaic from XVII century to modern times

In the XVII and XVIII centuries most of the artistic production in the field of mosaic develops itself around the decoration of St. Peter's Basilica.

Rome had never ceased to be a great center for the training of mosaicists, heirs of a great past, whom those who needed mosaic artworks had to adress to.

Artistic life in Rome was very active in the Baroque period. The opening of a glass-factory near the Vatican allowed new research and discoveries in the production of vitreous pastes.

63 THE OWL (XVII cent.)
Made for Cardinal Scipio Borghese. In the background are recognizable St. Peter's, the Forum and the Fontana Paola on the Janiculum Hill.
MARCELLO PROVENZALE, MUSEO DEGLI ARGENTI, FLORENCE

This is also the period of the invention of the "filato" technique and the subsequent production and diffusion of the *mosaico minuto*, that will become in the XVIII century the "new Roman art" par excellence. To this technique will be later dedicated the pages on the "Studio del Mosaico Vaticano" and "Mosaico Minuto and the Gran Tour".

The Roman mosaicists during the period 1600-1900 became not only largerly appreciated outside Rome, but also more scattered all over Europe, as to some of them was permitted to work for foreign patrons. So, during the XVIII century Roman master mosaicists are found not only in other Italian cities but *even in foreign countries*, some of which will try, as we will see, to open their own schools. Even the English architect Christopher Wren, during his sejourn in Italy, was inspired to apply mosaic in St. Paul's Cathedral, London, but then he was forced to abandon the idea. (The present mosaic are in fact of the XIX century).

Examples of Roman mosaics and their European influence during the period 1700-1900 are numberless. For now it is important to mention at least the *works of Marcello Provenzale, Mattia Moretti, Claudio Montecucchi, Francesco Belloni, Giacomo Raffaelli[5]*. And let us not forget the Russian scientist and literate *Mikhail V. Lomonosov* (1711-1765), whose art studio in St. Petersburg was directly inspired by the classical mosaic and the Studio Vaticano.

In the course of the XIX century, in which art in general is not precisely splendid, mosaicists were more occupied either with work of restoration or with faithful reproductions of pictures. By now they seem to lack the aspiration towards an autonomous art and to be happy with the executions of reproductions, always having in mind the long-held idea that mosaic must look like painting. The mosaic portrait of *King George IV*[6] is a stunning example of this trend, but who can deny its beauty even if a mere reproduction?[7]

Italian artists though, continued to receive commissions from all over the world. Entire families of mosaicists migrated to different countries where they also founded schools. We must remember London with the South Kensington Museum, the old denomination of what is today the Victoria and Albert Museum which opened a mosaic workshop whose artists contributed to several monuments, notably in the House of Parliament with the stories of St. George. To remain in the English ambit, but with work executed in Rome, worthy of mention are the mosaics of the *American Church of St. Paul's-within-the-walls*, in the Via Nazionale,

64
BATTLE OF THE
POLTAVA (XVIII cent.)
*Commemoration
of the victory of the Russian
Army over Charles XII
of Sweden (1709)*
M. LOMONOSOV,
ST. PETERSBURG, RUSSIA

65
NAPOLEON
BONAPARTE
(XIX cent.)
*Mosaic portrait
by F. Belloni, founder
of an atelier in Paris*

66 RECTANGULAR CONSOLLE TOP (cm 145x73)
Consolle with head of jupiter and very fine greek-key pattern
C. MONTECUCCHI, PALAZZO PITTI, FLORENCE

where the cartoons were drawn by the pre-raphaelite artist Sir Edward Burne-Jones. In the apse, the four Saints Ambrose, Patrick, Andrea and James bear the *portraits of four famous contemporaries*, namely J.P. Morgan, a wealthy benefactor of the church, General Ulysses Grant, Abraham Lincoln and *Giuseppe Garibaldi* who, we all know, was much loved by the English, many of which fought by his side in the battles of the Italian Risorgimento. The execution of the Pre-raphaelite mosaics were entrusted to the Venetian firm A. Salviati. The latter was an indefatigable promoter of the mosaic art, being both an artist and a business man (he was a lawyer by training). He is the one who first used the "indirect method" of applying the tesserae (see paragraph on "How is a mosaic made?") that allowed the pre-assemblage of the mosaic in the workshop, a quicker and less expensive technique. Salviati is also the one who transformed the craft into an industrial and commercial business much to detriment of the quality however. In 1851 appeared in the "Illustrated Exhibitor" a written account of the Great Exhibition at the Crystal Palace in London, mentioning the Roman mosaic "Tabletop by Barbieri" now in the Gilbert Collection.Another magnificent example of table-top is the one with the deeds of the *Greek hero Achilles* housed at Versailles.

69

70

67

82

Foreign countries too claimed their own laboratories: Russia, with Czar Nicholas I, wanted to open a school in Rome for Russian artists. The workshop was later transferred to St. Petersburg as a department of the Academy of Fine Arts, but unfortunately the school was closed in 1917 due to the tragic events of that year. A famous sample of the skill of this laboratory is the decoration of the *Church of St. Isaac, in St. Petersburg.*   *50*

Paris too had its own École, after the Restoration called "Manifacture Royale de la Mosaique". The works of the French mosaicists are to be seen everywhere in France, notably in the Church of the Sacré-Coeur in

67 ACHILLE'S SHIELD (XIX cent.)
Table top with stories of the Greek hero.
Gift of Pope Leo XII to Charle X of France
GRAND TRIANON, VERSAILLES

68 S. MICHAEL (XIX cent.)
Pre-raphaelite style, after the cartoons of
SIR EDWARD BURNE-JONES
CHURCH OF ST. PAUL'S-WITHIN-THE WALLS, ROME

69

THE CHRISTIAN WARRIORS
(XIX cent.)
*Detail of the bottom right side
of the Apse, where famous
personages can be recognized.
After the cartoons of
SIR EDWARD BURNE JONES,
CHURCH OF ST. PAUL'S-
WITHIN-THE WALLS, ROME*

70

DETAIL OF GARIBALDI'S
PORTRAIT

71
"TRUE" IMAGE
OF CHRIST
(XIX cent.)
*Icone
in the right
aisle
of St. Patrick's
Cathedral
NEW YORK
CITY*

Paris and Notre-Dame de la Garde in Marseille.

In our XX century we can trace two different trends. With the School of Spilimbergo in Friuli the mosaic production becomes even more industrial, with the cutting of the tesserae done by machine and with pre-assembled panels.

As already remarked, the result is often standardised and dull, with no life at all. Normally works like these are seen in bathrooms, swimming pools, entrances to underground passages and stations.

The other trend is the application of mosaics to the external façades of public buildings. Contemporary to the Salviati Firm, there was in Germany another important company called Wagner that produced both

smalti and mosaics. They were very instrumental in enlarging the utilisation of mosaic on *public buildings* such as banks, hospitals, city halls etc. *74 to 76*
Today mosaics are again used also for *interior decoration,* as for exemple in the bathroom. *72*

Mosaics applied to façades are always showing *very vivid colours* and *49* with large scale figures to give the *effect of modern painting.* *76*

A forerunner of the use of mosaics in architectural complexes was the Catalan architect Antonio Gaudi whose work appeared early this century in Barcelona, both in the Church of the Sagrada FamIlla and the baluster seats in the Guell Park where the artist made almost an orgiastic use of the coloured enamels, *marbles and stones.* His architecture looks like sculpture and he was among the first, in modern times, to *apply mosaic* *73* *to sculptured objets.*

Among the Italians, we owe to the painter Giorgio Severini the recommendation to use mosaics in public buildings. Born in Cortona, near Arezzo in 1883, Severini moved to Paris in 1906 where he came in contact with a circle of famous artists such as Amedeo Modigliani, Max Jacob,

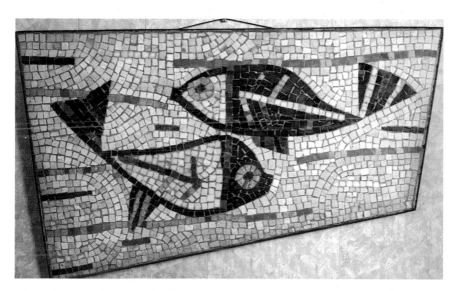

72 MOSAIC WITH FISH (Early '50s)
Embedded on a wooden panel of irregular rectangular shape.
Origin unknown.
PRIVATE COLLECTION

Leger, the Romanian Brancusi etc. He founded in Paris the Ecole d'Art italien and just before the second world war he received two great orders, that of the frescoes and mosaics for the University of Padua and the Foro Italico in Rome

The complex of the Foro Italico (former Foro Mussolini) was built between the years 1928 and 1937 and can be considered a great "village of sport". Architecturally speaking the complex evokes the past grandeur of Imperial Rome's edifices. The floor mosaics are in the *black and white figural style*, so much used in the floors of houses and public buildings of the first, second and third centuries in Rome. Some are white figures on a black background, others black figures on a white background.

The theme is of course that of sporting scenes, such as athletes intent on their daily practice, or aquatic scenes in the swimming pool etc. Severini's interest in mosaic art expressed itself also in articles and lectures given at Ravenna on the subject.

74
75

73
LA PEDRERA (XX cent.)
Roof-top sculpture
ANTONIO GAUDI,
BARCELONA, SPAIN

74-75
ATHLETES
(XX cent.)
*Black and white
mosaics
on the former
Piazzale
dell'Impero*
G. SEVERINI,
FORO ITALICO
(*former
Foro Mussolini*),
ROME

76 MOSES SAVED FROM THE WATERS (XX cent.),
MARC CHAGALL, ST. PAUL-DE-VANCE, FRANCE

Perhaps the largest works ever executed in mosaic in modern times are the ones in Mexico City, for the façades of the University Library and the Teatro de los Insurgentes, completed around year 1952. Another large mosaic panel is the one called *"The Golden Rule"* by the American artist Norman Rockwell, property of the U.N. Headquarter in New York. *104*

The list of modern mosaics could go on for quite a while. They are found *in every part of the world today.*

We want to end though our short story by mentioning the Monument *71* to Pinocchio at Collodi, Tuscany. The artist is Venturino Venturi who on a low, undulating wall surrounding an open courtyard on the hills tells us the story of the famous marionette-boy in simple, brightly coloured scenes.

NOTES

[5] M.Moretti (birth date unknown), among the first mosaicists to work for the Reverenda Fabrica di S.Pietro in the first-half of the XVIII cent. F.Belloni (1772-1843), became a mosaicist against his family's advice, as they were rather well-off. G.Raffaelli (1753-1836),considered the initiator of micromosaic art. Much admired by the King of Poland who bestowed on him a noble title. He is buried in the Polish Church of St.Stanislav at Rome.

[6] King George IV was quite unpopular due to his private life and excessive expenses.His reign saw the emancipation of the Irish Catholics during the premiership of the Duke of Wellington.The original painting of the King was executed with great technical skill by the last of the great British portrait painters Sir T.Lawrence.

[7] Certainly a contemporary artist would opt for a re-interpretation of the subject in his/her own way.But in the first half of 1800, mosaic art was still under the spell of the XV cent.,embraced by the academicians of the time.

---

on the following pages:

77 VESTAL (XIX cent.)
by the mosaicist Clemente Ciuli, active in Rome in the first half of XIX cent. He is remembered as one of the best artists in the micromosaic technique. MUSÉE DU JARDIN DES PLANTES, PARIS

78 VIEW OF THE ROMAN FORUM (Early XIX cent.)
Micromosaic broach mounted on gold. PRIVATE COLLECTION

Expansion
and
Techniques

- 6 -

Studio del Mosaico Vaticano

The importance of the Vatican School is such that we must dedicate to it an entire chapter. Its institution dates back to about 1578. This is the time in fact when Pope Gregory XIII Boncompagni expressed the desire to decorate the four chapels of the cross-vault of St. Peters' Basilica. Pope Gregory XIII was a great pontiff, patron of both arts and sciences. During his reign he reformed the calendar and founded the Vatican Astronomical Observatory, among other things.

Therefore the beginning of a stable and continuous activity for the decoration of the Basilica dates back to the end of the XVI century and continues for nearly three centuries with moments of rest.

The Reverenda Fabbrica Pontificia del Mosaico as the Studio was called was under the direct supervision of Girolamo Muziano, academician at St. Luca who also furnished the cartoons for the decoration of the Gregorian Chapel, the first of the four chapels to be decorated.

In this regard, the Vatican sent a request to the Republic of Venice, that is demanding the supply of four master-mosaicists. This request reveals the initial dependence of Rome on Venice, not only for the creative executors of the work, but also for the supplies of the materials to be used. The lagoon city was then the undisputed centre of production of vitreous pastes. Some years later though, around 1630, due to the terrible epidemics that decimated its population, Venice remained without its famous masters and we witness the opposite fact, that is an artist leaves from Rome for Venice. His name is Leopoldo da Pozzo to whom was entrusted the task of creating a new school and to carry on with new works for the Basilica of St. Mark.

The decoration of the four chapels of the cross-vault of St. Peter's constitutes the first great phase of the activity of the Vatican Studio, followed later by the Cupola of Michelangelo and those of the lateral aisles. On page 99 is given the chronological order of the executions of the mosaics in the Basilica.

The second phase coincides with the reproduction of the oil paintings above the altars. Why this? The degree of humidity in the Basilica was such as to prove devastating for the well-being of the canvases. In

79 S. MICHAEL ARCHANGEL (XVII cent.)
Mosaicist of the Vatican School Calandra, after the cartoon
of Cavalier d'Arpino.
CATHEDRAL OF MACERATA, MARCHE, ITALY

order to save them it was suggested their removal from the Basilica and placement in safer places. Subsequently all the pictures were to be replaced with mosaic reproductions.

However among the various ranks of the Church, and among the experts, not everybody agreed with this solution, and the various conflicts of opinion certainly were the cause for the delay with which the substitution took place.

Around year 1627 though a first attempt for the replacement of all the altar-pieces was carried on. Cavalier d'Arpino painted a Saint Michael the Archangel over Lucifer, to be placed in the homonymous chapel. It was then *reproduced in mosaic* by the fine master mosaicist *G.B. Calandra,* but even if the work pleased the Pope Urban VIII, Barberini, who was very devout to the Archangel Michael, the plan for the displacement of the paintings was postponed to an indeterminate date. The mosaic is kept today in the Cathedral of Macerata, in the Italian region of the Marches.

The major problem for the substitution was given by the very nature of the Venetian enamels that were very glossy and so transparent that depending on the incidence of light they changed their colour accordingly. This translucence and variability of the colour was good for the central and the lateral cupolas, but resulted as unsuitable for the altarpieces where the mosaics had to be assimilated with the paintings, what really they wanted to achieve for St. Peters. In fact the assimilation had to deceive the observer, who even from a very close distance had to believe he was admiring an oil painting and not a mosaic. The dominant motive of the Vatican mosaics in fact was the very same of Vasari's, that is "pittura per l'eternità".

Along with the decoration of the cupolas, the Reverenda Fabbrica was promoting research aimed at finding new mixtures for the vitreous pastes. This is the moment when several furnaces were opened in the area near the Vatican, hoping to escape the Venetian monopoly. By trial and error finally success attended a Roman "fornaciaro" (glass-maker), the genial Alessio Mattioli, who with his own batches could finally obtain opaque vitreous pastes in a very large range of colours. The new opaque paste was called "scorzetta" (rind). Opacity was important because it stopped the incidence of the light on the colour, and therefore permitted the realisation of a mosaic much *more similar to an oil painting,* mistaken for such even at a very close distance.

In the second half of the XVII century Rome was able to produce its own enamels and escape the Venetian monopoly. This was of course an

80 BUTTERFLIES AND LYRE (XVIII cent.)
Micromosaic, probably by Giacolo Raffaelli.
PRIVATE COLLECTION

enormous economic advantage. Just to give you an idea of the variety of enamels at the disposal of the Vatican mosaicist, they assembled a provision of 28.000 chromatic varieties (as opposed to the barely fifty shades used in Santa Maria Maggiore in the 5th century) kept in 10.000 drawers. Some lots are still the remnants of the '700 vitreous pastes.

The replacement of the altar-pieces with mosaics lasted for the entire XVIII century until mid-XX cent. On the *Plan of St. Peter's Basilica* and on the following page is given the chronology of the replacements.

81

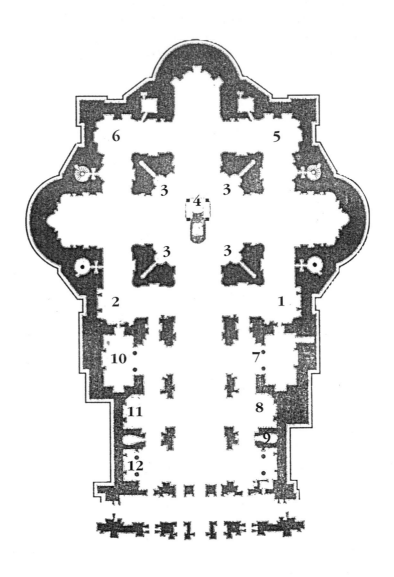

81   *Plan of St. Peter's Basilica*

Chronology of the executions of the mosaics
in the various parts of the Basilica

It must be noted that often the authors of the cartoons were well known artists. The names of the various Popes are also given.

1 - Gregorian Chapel after the cartoons of G. Muziano
(Gregory XIII, Boncompagni)   1578-80

2 - Pendentives of the major cupola (Michelangelos)
after the cartoons of Giovanni de' Vecchi and Cesare Nebbia
(Clement VIII, Aldobrandini)   1598-99

3 - Clementine Chapel after the cartoons of Pomarancio
(Clement VIII, Aldobrandini)   1601-02

4 - *Inner Cupola* of Michelangelo after the *cartoons of*   *82*
Cavalier d'Arpino (Clement VIII, Aldobrandini;
Leo XI, Medici; Paul V, Borghese)   1603-12

5 and 6 - The other two chapels of the cross vault after
the cartoons of Lanfranco, A.Sacchi and R. Romanelli
(This artist was later active in France, on request of
Cardinal Mazarin who charged him with work at his
palace and the Louvre) (Paul V, Borghese;
Gregory XV, Ludovisi; Urban VIII, Barberini).   1610-48

7 - Vestibule of the Blessed Sacrament Chapel

8 - Vestibule of the Chapel of St. Sebastian

9 - Vestibule of the Chapel of the Crucifix
(Innocent X, Pamphili; Alexander VII, Chigi)   1653-63

10 - Vestibule of the Choir Chapel after the cartoons of Maratta
(Innocent XII, Pignatelli; Clement XI, Albani)   1699-1721

11 - Vestibule of the Chapel of the Presentation
(Clement XI, Albani; Innocent XIII, Conti;
Benedict XIII, Orsini)   1720-29

12 - Vestibule of the Baptisimal Font after the cartoons
of Francesco Trevisani (Benedict XIII, Orsini; Clement XII,
Corsini; Benedict XIV, Lambertini)   1724-46

Chronology of the Replacement of the altar-pieces

I-IV	The four altar-pieces of the Grotte from original of Andrea Sacchi (Urban VIII, Barberini)	1628-89
V	Martyrdom of SS. Processus and Martinian by Valentin (Clement XI, Albani)	1709
VI	The Navicella by Lanfranco (Innocent XIII, Conti)	1721
VII	Presentation of Mary at the Temple by Romanelli (Benedict XIII, Orsini)	1726-28
VIII	Martyrdom of S. Petronilla By Guercino (Clement XII, Corsini)	1728-30
IX	Communion of St. Jerome by Domenichino (Clement XII, Corsini)	1730-33
X	The Baptism of Christ by Maratta (Clement XII, Corsini)	1732-34
XI	Martyrdom of St.Sebastian (Clement XII, Corsini)	1733-36
XII	St.Peter baptistes the Roman Centurion Cornelius by Procaccini (Clement XII, Corsini)	1733-36
XIII	Baptism of SS. Processus and Martinian by Passeri (Clement XII, Corsini)	1736-37
XIV	Martyrdom of S. Erasmo by Poussin (Clement XII, Corsini)	1737-39
XV	King Venceslao from Bohemia by Caroselli (Clement XII, Corsini)	1739-40
XVI	Immaculate Conception by Bianchi (Benedict XIV, Lambertini)	1743-55
XVII	Mass of St. Basil by Subleyras (Benedict XIV, Lambertini)	1748-51
XVIII	Healing of the crippled man by Mancini (Benedict XIV, Lambertini)	1751-58
XIX	St. Michael Archangel by Reni (Benedict XIV, Lambertini)	1757-58
XX	Resurrection of the Tabita by Costanzo (Clement XIII, Rezzonico)	1758-60
XXI	The Transfiguration by Raphael (Clement XIII, Rezzonico)	1759-67
XXII	Mass of St.Gregory by Sacchi (Clement XIV, Ganganelli)	1770-72
XXIII	Crucifiction of St.Peters by Reni (Pius VI, Braschi)	1782
XXIV	Ecstasy of St. Francis by Domenichino (Pius VI, Braschi; Pius VII, Chiaramonti)	1795-1801
XXV	Deposition from the Cross by Caravaggio	

82 MICHELANGELO'S INNER CUPOLA (early XVII cent.)
After the cartoons of Cavalier d'Arpino
ST. PETER'S BASILICA, VATICAN CITY

Some of the original paintings were transferred in 1727 to Urbino. Some hang in the Pinacoteca Vaticana and in the Basilica of St. Maria degli Angeli in Rome.

The location of the Vatican studio has changed several times. Originally a small room called "of St. Gregory" near the Clementine Chapel in St. Peters, afterwards being housed in some other spaces and warehouses of the Reverenda Fabrica, founding subsequently a more permanent accommodation in the nearby foundry where Bernini himself had cast his own bronzes.

During the French occupation of Rome, the Studio had its premises in Palazzo of S. Uffizio, then with the Restoration moved once more to

83 HIS HOLINESS POPE JOHN PAUL II PRESENTING PRESIDENT AND MRS CLINTON TWO MOSAIC-PICTURES ON OCCASION OF THEIR OFFICIAL VISIT.

Palazzo Giraud in the Borgo (the quarter that since early medieval times had developed around the Basilica), returning later within the Vatican precincts in a gallery near S. Damaso Courtyard, from where one could gain access from a stairway that still today is called "staircase of the Mosaic".

A recent location behind the apse of St.Peters' on the west side of the present St. Martha's Square has been demolished to make room for a large underground parking place. Today its location, is on the other side of Santa Martha square, in a newly restored building.

The Vatican Mosaic Studio is still active in the present day. The works produced by its mosaicists are to be found all over the world. The production is normally done in the Studio, as well as the mounting of the single panels, and from there shipped to their final destinations. Parishes, governments, public bodies and private people alike are the many recipients. Just to name one, in the Shrine of the Immaculate Conception in Washington D.C. there is a picture of the Blessed Mother that has been made by today's Vatican artists.

A very well established custom[1] is that whenever a distinguished person is received in private audience, the Holy Father presents him/her with a mosaic picture, either of a religious image or any other appropriate subject. In recent times Pope John Paul II presented President Clinton with two mosaics, one showing the map of the Unites States of America and the other a view of the Forum with the Colosseum in the background. Tradition goes on.

83

NOTES

82

[1] There are records that in the past centuries popes presented mosaics to princes and emperors. The most famous is The Double Portrait of Emperor Joseph II and his brother Duke Leopold of Tuscany after the oil painting of Pompeo Batoni, now in the Kunsthistorisches Museum in Vienna commissionned by Pope Clement XIV.

---

on the following page:

84   PERSIAN SYBIL (XVIII cent.)
Perhaps after the cartoon of Guido Reni. Executed in Rome as a gift presented by the Corsini Family to the Granduke of Tuscany Leopold.
MATTIA MORETTI, GALLERIA DEGLI UFFIZI, FLORENCE

- 7 -

Mosaico Minuto
and the Grand Tour

Already by year 1680, but especially during the XVIII and early XIX centuries, it grew more and more popular amongst the members of the North-European ruling class to indulge their interest in travelling to the South of Europe.

These journeys were undertaken with several purposes in mind: to acquire manners and languages, to admire the remains of the classical past and not least to collect art and antiquities. We all know too well how many pieces of art from the classical countries form today either private or public collections in countries such as England, France and Germany.

The tour could last months or years, especially if the person stayed longer not only to visit but to study. Many milords embarked on the so called Grand Tour before settling down to their duties and marriage in their own country.

In London the Società dei Dilettanti was also founded, formed of people who had been on the Grand Tour and who in their periodical gatherings discussed their experiences, findings and who knows, perhaps... misfortunes.

The road to Italy if the Grand Tourist came from the British Isles passed necessary through France. Once reached Paris, the journey continued on to Lyon, over the Alps by the Mont Cenis Pass, then Genua and from there to various destinations of the peninsula.

Tourists (as it is also the case today) always wanted to buy souvenirs to take home as a tangible reminder of a trip that perhaps had opened to them new vistas of people, places and life in general. Certainly many of these people must have gone back home truly changed.

Not only antiquity but also local crafts impressed the foreign visitor, and the choice of what to buy was indeed large. Exemples of artworks executed by mosaicists of the Studio Vaticano could be found *in every major Italian city*: a choice of them was given in the previous pages.

63, 66 80, 84

The city of Genua was famous for its velvets and laces, Venice offered multi-coloured glass in sparkling tones, Florence was renowned

85   IL CARRO DELL'AMORE (Chariot with Cupids) (XIX cent.)
Mosaico Minuto table-top. SALA PIO V, VATICAN MUSEUM

for the pietre dure and for the Doccia dinner services, while Naples captured the tourist with the skillfully carved cameos and corals.

78, 85
86 What about Rome? *Mosaico minuto* was the most sought-after *object d'art* of the time by the discerning traveller in Rome during the XIX century. In fact the craft of the mosaic never died in the Eternal city. A month would not be enough time to visit churches, ancient buildings and museums where it is possible to admire mosaics that span from antiquity to modern times (see suggested itineraries at the end of the book).

In the second half of the XVIII century, the mosaic decoration of St. Peters Basilica was moving slowly towards its conclusion. Work became scarce for the many mosaicists and the Vatican studio was presented with

86
CLOCK (XIX cent.)
Micromosaic, rare marble,
pietre dure and bronze
by G. Raffaelli
(Permission of F. Partridge)

the problem of finding new ways to keep the mosaicists occupied and still able to earn their living.

Pope Pius VI tried to help out by commissioning antependia in mosaic for the altars of St.Peter. But the Vatican finances were not too florid at the time. Another boost came from the decision to decorate with mosaic the altars of the Cathedral of Loreto.[2]

It is in this period that a number of Roman mosaicists accept the invitation of foreign sponsors either to work for them or to open schools abroad. Moving abroad was always subject to a special dispensation granted by the Pope. In fact there was always a certain reticence in granting it for fear that "the secret" of the Vatican Studio technique would be divulged too easily. It is for example then that on request of the Russian painter and poet *Mikhail Lomonosov* was opened a studio in St. Petersburg connected with the Imperial Academy of Fine Arts. With the death of the artist unfortunately the studio was closed and only enjoyed a short revival a century later thanks to the mosaicist Michelangelo Barberi, but also this second attempt ceased in 1917 at the eve of the Russian revolution.

We have already mentioned that in England a studio was opened

64

87 LAST SUPPER (XIX cent.)
After the original fresco by Leonardo da Vinci.
Executed in Milan by Giacomo Raffaelli
MINORITEN KIRCHE, VIENNA, AUSTRIA

under the care of the South Kensington Museum, which did not have unfortunately a long life.

France too opened a school. Pope Pius IX in person granted his permission for the opening of the Ecole Nationale de la Mosaique, where young deaf-mutes were trained in the art.

During the Napoleonic occupation of Milan a studio was created in imitation of the Vatican one by command of Prince Eugene Beauharnais. The most famous work executed in this studio by the mosaicist Giacomo Raffaelli in 1804 was a *copy of Leonardo's Last Supper* which is now kept in the Minoritenkirche in Vienna[3] (reproduced here thanks to the kind permission of Father Nicola).

Other mosaicists who remained in Rome started to detach themselves from the Vatican Studio and open up their own private workshops. These were mainly to be found in tourist areas with the major concentration around the Spanish Steps, as for example that of *Clemente Ciuli*.

The Spanish Steps is a world-known site where at that time people not only visited but sojourned for long periods. In the vicinity in fact, on Via del Corso, lived Goethe and the English poet Keats rented a room in a house just attached to the Spanish Steps, today the Keats and Shelley Memorial House. These are just the most illustrious guests in Rome

87

77

88 TEMPLE OF THE SYBIL (XVIII cent.)
Very fine mosaico minuto with view of temple, cascades and countryside.
PRIVATE COLLECTION, ROME

89 TEMPLE OF MINERVA MEDICA (XVIII cent.)
Ruins still seen in Rome. Broach mounted on "rosso antico" marble.
PRIVATE COLLECTION, ROME

among the many others. Drinking tea at Babington's Tea Rooms or shopping around in the antique shops and mosaic workshops was and still is certainly part of the fun.

It is well documented that by year 1820 there were about 20 micromosaicists active in Rome.

This coincided with the magic moment of the so called "mosaico minuto" and the utilisation of the "smalti filati", an invention ascribed to *Giacomo Raffaelli* whom we have seen was later active in the newly opened *studio in Milan.*

80, 86
87

Smalti filati (or glass filaments) are obtained by warming in an open flame a small lump of coloured glass that under the action of the heat becomes malleable and can be stretched (filato) in thickness from that of a piece of string to the finest cotton threads.

This operation resulted in obtaining long rods that could be reduced in very tiny (minute)tesserae. These were then assembled with the help of tweezers on a mount of stone or glass to create beautiful scenes which were later applied to objects-d'art or fine jewellery. Any spaces were filled with coloured wax and then polished off. The finest micro-mosaics of the late XVIII century can contain up to 1400 tesserae per square inch (2.54 cm).

In this book it would be too long to list the names of these micromosaicists but they are all well documented in the Vatican School Archives. We must mention here the Castellani firm which reached great fame above all for the re-interpretation of Christian and Byzantine mosaics in their jewellery. This Rome based firm had been founded in 1814 by Fortunato Pio Castellani and was active until the late 1870's. Not only their Roman shop was visited by the discerning customer, but also those of London and Paris with their international affluent clientele. The firm's presence in international exhibitions helped in strengthening their reputation which was admittedly based on an impeccable research and study of ancient original jewels, coupled with great skill and taste in the reproduction and the re-interpretation of ancient masterpieces.

As the objects bought by tourists were to be transported, normally they were modest in size, mostly were objects for personal use.

The subjects reproduced in the mosaics reveal either the re-born interest towards *classical myths* such as the Apollo of Belvedere and the Laocoon, both works in the Vatican Museum, and themes such as tripods, craters, heads of statues, the unfailing *Pliny's Doves*, probably the most copied subject of all.

66, 67, 85

10

With the dawning of the Romantic view towards life, objets-d'art such as snuff-boxes, bracelets, broaches, paper-weights etc. reproduce architectural ruins, *views of the Roman Forum*, the Cestia Pyramid and of course the Colosseum and the Pantheon. Also popular genre scenes such as people dressed in local costumes or shown as they dance and drink (*see back cover*), *small pets* etc. were commonly an inspiration for the artists.

78

90

These micro-mosaics are today found in antique shops, and at times they appear at public auctions becoming thus *part of private collections*. The largest private collection is the one formed by Mr and Mrs Arthur Gilbert of Beverly Hills, California. It has been for a while on view in the Los Angeles County Museum of Art, at present though is stored in London at Somerset House on the Strand, waiting for its final home in the rooms of this house, already home of the famous Courtauld Institute with its collection of French Impressionist and Post-impressionist paintings. As far as it is known this display though will not be ready until the end of the Millennium.

88, 89

Public collections of micro-mosaics can be seen in the Hermitage Museum St. Petersburg, Russia, with its relatively comprehensive collection, and in the Vatican Museums. To those visiting the latter we recommend a visit in the room at the end of the Gallery of maps, in order to get a good idea of the work.

NOTES

[20] Another great work met by the Vatican Studio in the XIX Century was the decoration of the Basilica of St. Paul's outside-the-walls, half-destroyed by a fire.
[21] The Minoritenkirche in Vienna is the Italian Church of the Madonna della Neve.

90
COCKER SPANIEL
(XIX cent.)
Mosaico minuto pendant mounted on Victorian pinchbeck.
PRIVATE COLLECTION
ROME

- 8 -

*H*ow is a Mosaic made?

Mosaic, as like any art, was not perfect from its inception, and has of course evolved throughout the centuries both in technique and materials.

A very short description would be "the art of creating patterns and figures by assembling in a bed of cement or other binding materials, variously sized fragments of coloured marble, stones, glass, mother-of-pearl, precious stones etc." Generally speaking therefore the technique falls in the category of inlay.

No doubt its durability and value depended on the quality of the various materials employed and on the skilled craftsmanship of the workmen.

91 *Mosaicists at work.*

During the classical period, apart from some passages in Vitruvius' "On Architecture" not much has been found written on this art, and we have to wait until Diocletian's "Edict on Prices" (301 A.D.) to find more information, at least on the various names and tasks of the workmen and the wages paid to them. They were normally paid on a daily base.

According to the allotment of specific tasks, the Roman artisans can be classified as follows:

<u>Pictor imaginarius</u>, who created the cartoon and suggested the colour in the case of coloured mosaics. He received the top wage of 175 sesterces a day

<u>Pictor parietarius</u>, who transferred the cartoon onto the pavement or wall, enlarging it according to the actual surface to be decorated. He earned about 75 sesterces a day.

<u>Calcis Coctor</u>, who prepared the cement. His wage was roughly 60 sesterces a day

<u>Pavimentarius</u>, who prepared the bed or surface on which the mosaic was to be set

<u>Tessellarius</u>, who was concerned with the simplest parts of the mosaic

<u>Musearius</u>, who executed the most complex parts and also the figures.

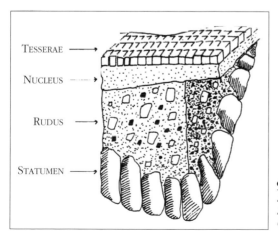

TESSERAE

NUCLEUS

RUDUS

STATUMEN

92
SKETCH OF THE VARIOUS STRATA OF A MOSAIC FLOOR

Each of these three earned the average sum of 50-60 sesterces a day.

We are certain then from documentary evidence that the execution of mosaics needed group work, above all when the decoration was ambitious in scale. Mosaics therefore were an expensive art to produce.

A very clear pictorial description of the diverse functions of the artisans can be detected from a bas-relief in the Archaeological Museum at Ostia (Rome): two porters carry sacks of material, while others prepare the bed and cut the tesserae, all working under the supervision of the master mosaicist.

It is also possible that the artisans formed itinerant teams moving from place to place where the work was to be executed.

The close examination of the surviving physical evidence is however what helps most to understand how mosaics were produced. Pavements were done in situ. We can imagine that for large pavements both the pavimentarius and the tessellarius worked on their knees or squatted down. Only the central panel, if any, was done separately and inserted later. This was called emblema (from the Greek word emballo- to put inside). The emblemata were normally set on a tray of stone or terracotta. Their quality was normally very high and this of course added to the cost and subsequent value of the mosaics.

Cheaper mosaics made use of pseudo-emblemata, whereas the central panel was not detachable.

Pavements had to be walked on and therefore required a strong foundation, which needed building skills, and in fact Vitruvius treats *92* mosaic as just a simple branch of the building trade. A simple *sketch* can give an idea of the various strata.

The first step was to dig the ground about 50 cm. deep. The bottom was then well pressed and consolidated with wooden planks, then covered with a thick rubble bedding (*statumen*) followed by a layer of coarse mortar (*rudus*) and finally by a finer layer of cement in which the tesserae were to be embedded. The interstices between the tesserae were filled with mortar and grout (liquid mortar) and the final touch consisted in the levelling and polishing of the surface with sand and water.

93, 96 They also used a large number of *border ornaments* for different floor designs.

Marbles and rocks did not have to be too hard or too soft, so that the cutting was easy and the colours too remained unchanged with the course of time.

114

In Ancient Greece existed numerous quarries of very high quality marbles. For their part, the Romans imported as much material as they wanted from the remotest parts of their empire, plus the travertine quarries of Tivoli were an inexhaustible source of material from which obtain mortar. In the Middle Ages the very same edifices of the Eternal City were dilapidated and became quarries of marble which was transported to far distant places such as Kiev and Aquisgrana.

In the Roman world, according to the nature of the tesserae (sometimes also called abaculi from the Greek word abakischoi) and their dimension, several techniques were distinguished. The technique is referred to as "opus":

Opus incertum — when both the cut and the setting of the tesserae is made in a casual way at random

Opus scutulatum — among the tesserae of the same colour are inserted others of various sizes and colours (it was first used for the floor of the Temple of Jupiter on the Capitoline Hill). However since the term "scutula" means romboid, this opus also refers to floor with romboic shaped tiles

Opus signinum — from Segni, floors made with pieces of stones and crushed potsherd. It was a very economic pavement to produce.

Opus tesselatum — mosaic made with tesserea of regular size and colour, used particularly for natural background or simple ornament

Opus segmentatum — insertion of larger tesserae of the same colour in an opus tesselatum

Opus vermiculatum — made up of tesserae of small dimension and cut with great precision. A technique used above all for the more expensive emblemata or pictorial inserts.

Opus musivum — technique used to decorate walls and vaults, using above all vitreous pastes. In the modern language the term "musivum" has a larger connotation of a mosaic work done in different techniques.

The above definitions of names have sometimes been mixed, but it serves as a rough guide.

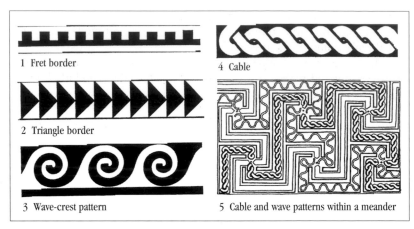

93 VARIOUS DESIGNS OF MOSAIC PATTERNS.

1 Fret border

2 Triangle border

3 Wave-crest pattern

4 Cable

5 Cable and wave patterns within a meander

With the transition from floor to wall mosaics, contemporaneously with the passage from pagan to Christian world, some adaptation of the basic foundation had to be worked out.

For example, emblemata were not much used in Christian mosaics but it should be remarked here that the bust of Christ in the apse of St. John Lateran was embedded as an emblema and this gave rise to the belief that the head had been transported there miraculously (the mosaics were completely replaced in 1884 under Leo XIII).

Also the nave mosaics of Santa Maria Maggiore were made on independent beds, in the manner of emblemata. In a sense though, in the Christian mosaics the artisan was freer to adapt a looser approach to the setting of the tesserae, as the texture did not have to be very compact as necessary for the pavements.

At the time of Emperor Justinian, artists had already at their disposal pictorial schemes, that is prototypes that had become well established. The designs drawn on the plaster were never therefore invented in situ. The theme to be represented, as it later happened for fresco decoration, was dictated by ecclesiastics of high rank.

The way the mosaics were to be read often depended on the architectural design of the church itself and it is always possible to trace a hierarchical order and place.

Walls and vaults as observed in the Byzantine and Venetian mosaics were covered with three different layers of mortar (in the church of S. Vitale at Ravenna four different layers have been counted) before the actual embedding of the tesserae.

The mortar was applied to the wall in several stages. First the brick wall was covered with a coarser layer of mortar which included aggregates of sand and crushed bricks, and then clamps or flat-headed iron nails were nailed in it to reinforce the surface, above all on the domes. The first coat as well the second one of a finer mortar were roughened so that the last layer could better adhere to them. Also there is evidence that a waterproofing agent such as bitumen, tar or resin was applied to the wall before applying the first coarser layer of mortar. Each layer was allowed time to dry and harden, and then was moistened again when the next layer was to be applied, in order to obtain a better bond.

The final (third or fourth) coat was normally applied a little at a time so that it always remained soft throughout the application of the tesserae. Normally the final thickness of the coats did not exceed three inches. In Byzantine works often the mortar was laid in an undulating manner to create irregularities on the surface to obtain specific effects. The undulations create effects of depth to the gold tesserae which otherwise would appear very flat and reduce the modelling of the figures to silhouettes.

Only a certain amount of work could be done in a day (that was a "giornata") and with a close look it is possible to discern the seams between the one day's work and the next.

The plaster itself was a mixture of lime, normally travertine from quarries on the outskirts of Rome, powdered marble, pozzolana (volcanic stone) with sometime the addition of straw and even cow dung!

From the quality of the plaster depended the duration of the mosaic so that this was a very delicate moment in the development of the work. Documents tell us that at a certain point the authorities of Venice forbade the shooting of fireworks and crackers during solemn ceremonies because at every detonation a little bit of the mosaics of St. Mark's detached itself from the wall!

When the master mosaicists of St.Peter's Basilica, Girolamo Muziano from Brescia, was working in the Cappella Gregoriana, he evolved a mastic containing oil, this being known as "oil putty". The basic ingredients, mixed in different measures, were powered travertine (60%), slaked lime, also from travertine (25%) and then the addition of both raw (10%) and boiled linseed oil (5%). This mixture of oil putty permitted the surface to stay as long as possible moistened and soft.

A sound foundation was then indispensable for the subsequent inlaying of the tesserae. What kind of material were they made of?

Materials could be very different. From pebbles to marble chips, from shells to mother-of-pearl and precious stones too such as lapis lazuli, malachite and turquoise, cornelian, jasper etc. just to name a few. We understand that the Aztecs even used perishable materials such as birds feathers for their mosaics! However for walls and vaults the material par excellence was glass or smalto (glass obtained by a melting process), also referred to as *vitreous paste* or with an inaccurate term "enamels".

In Italy the supremacy in the production of glass was held by the city of Venice, but we have seen that in the XVII century there was a great boost of local furnaces in Rome favoured by the Vatican for reasons already explained.

97

94
WOOD-FIRED
"BEEHIVE" FURNACE
of the Venetian type.
*Illustration
from "De Re metallica"
by G. Agricola (1494-1555)
published posthumously
in 1556.*

As for Venice, to be more precise from around the year 1292, the glass was produced on the small island of Murano, where the Venetian glass-makers were forced to move and work because of the danger from the furnaces fires to the city itself. They used *wood fired beehive furnaces*.

Research in the field proves that often glass was also produced locally, as in the case of Orvieto during the time of the decoration of the Cathedral, as well as a furnace in the nearby locality of Monteleone. In the east, a well established centre for the production of mosaic glass was the city of Kiev.

The local furnaces were normally not too far from the place where the mosaics were being made. In other cases, itinerant merchants from Venice visited their clients and supplied them with the needed materials.

Both the component of the batch and the temperature at which the mixture is fused (at about 1200°-1500° centigrades) was of primary importance in order to get high quality glass. The whole process of melting the glass takes about 12 hours, after which the liquid mass is scooped in round metal plates so as to obtain a sort of pancake shapes (known as "pizzas") which are then cooled down. Also the cooling process is quite lengthy, from 4 to 12 hours. The thickness of the "pizzas" can vary from 10 mm to 15,20 mm, but some can be as thin as 3 mm.

The pizzas are then broken down into the shapes of tesserac by the artist in his studio, and to this purpose are employed a series of different tools, such as mosaic hammer, files, glass cutters, palette knives, tweezers, nippers: each tool used according to the operation to be performed.

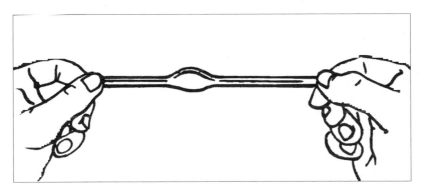

95 "MAKING FILATI" (OR THREADS)

Nowadays ready cut-to-size tesserae can be obtained directly from the supplying factories. The standard size of a tessera is about 13x10 mm.

A mention of the smalti filati and miniature tesserae was made when writing about the works of the Studio del Mosaico Vaticano. The smalti filati is indeed an invention of a "fornaciaro" (glassmaker) of the Vatican factory, Giacomo Raffaelli. The Vatican factory was closed early this century, but the Studio is still one of the few workshop to hold a full range of thousands of shades, all perfectly catalogued and stored in appropriate drawers. The filato was probably a by-product obtained in the search for the minute tesserae to be used to emulate the shades of colour in the paintings.

In the Vatican factory the glass was scooped in square plates, becoming in effect square tablets bearing the Pope's mark. Filato means "thread", and the process consists in removing a lump of the material from the tablet and melting it over an open flame and then drawing it up to resemble threads (fili) of different width. Glass is not a good conductor of heat and therefore both the lump and the strip obtained *can be held in the fingers* reasonably close to the flame without risk of burning. The threads or fili need some time to cool and harden and at this point can be clipped into minute sizes.

Smalti filati were greatly employed in the production of portable objets-d'art, jewellery etc. all in great demand by the Grand Tourists in Rome in the XVIII and XIX centuries.

In the Byzantine mosaics, gold glass was much used, either for entire backgrounds or for part of them especially to represent the halos of Christ and the Saints and to emulate the effect of supernatural light. But gold tesserae have also been found in floor mosaics, at Villa Adriana and at Aquileia, to name but two locations.

In the course of time there have been slightly different processes and methods evolved to obtain gold glass, but basically the gold foil is, so to say, sandwiched between a film of thin and a thick layer of ordinary glass. Real 24 carat gold is employed in the gold glass and needless to say, this results in an expensive material. If the top or the lower layer of glass is tinted, gold glass can appear in different nuances. For example, a yellow base will enhance the gold's brilliance, while a red tint will give to it a warm effect, and so forth. In order to save money, sometimes the gold was replaced by copper and the silver, in case of silver glass, by tin; but of course the result is never as brilliant.

For the actual execution of the mosaic a rough outline of the design

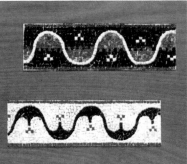
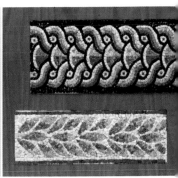

96 FURTHER DESIGNS OF CLASSICAL MOTIFS
a) Meander of swastikas; b) Wave patterns; c) Floral pattern

was made on the wall, but this phase was always followed by the full colour design, using the red in the place of gold in the background (as seen in the *Christ as "Helios" in the Vatican Scavi*).

102

The painting served as a guide to the mosaicists, but also to tone down the plaster. The colour of the design remained visible in the interstices of the tesserae and the effect resulted in the enhancement of the colour of all the mosaic when this was finished.

Towards the end of the XIII century, and the beginning of the XIX century, a cartoon was used together with the sinopia on the wall.

A cartoon is a drawing on strong paper, usually full size and did not need to be too elaborate. The sinopia is the underpainting as a preparatory drawing for the mosaics (and also for a fresco). The name is derived from Sinope in Asia Minor, a city famous for the red pigment often used for the purpose. When applying the tesserae a skilled mosaicist always keeps in mind the so called *andamento* that is the flow of the tesserae that should always follow the direction of the brush strokes on the cartoon.

91

For the decoration of churches, as they by necessity included sacred representation, the artists did not have a free hand in the composition, but had to conform to established conventions. In this, they were helped either by textbooks or iconographic guides plus the collection of sketches that each artist certainly owned of the most recurrent motifs. This procedure was used above all when the artists worked without cartoons.

If the cartoons were smaller than the real mosaic composition it was necessary to enlarge them on the wall, the enlarged design always maintaining the proportions of the original. Photographic enlargements can be used today, but in the past the operation was more elaborate indeed.

In Ravenna today a technique is used which consists in tracing on paper the major lines, which are afterwards retraced in ink of the reverse of the paper. When the paper is laid on the moistened surface of the plaster, the ink lines will be imprinted on the wall.

The actual setting of the tesserae on the surface can be done by a direct, indirect or reciprocal setting.

The "classical" and most natural is doubtless the direct method where the tesserae are embedded one by one. In this method the mosaicist's energy is really infused in the work. At this stage he can really be very creative and use at best his/her inventiveness. In this method the tesserae never result in being set in the same position or angle of inclination. The light that touches these tesserae is reflected in a myriad of shimmering lights which change with every movement of the viewer.

In the indirect or reverse method, the tesserae are glued face downward on the paper or canvas bearing the design. If the mosaic is of large proportions, the design is "dismembered" and then when the paper or canvas bearing the glued tesserae is pushed into the plaster, great care is needed in order to reassemble it. The paper or canvas now covering the surface is removed by using water. Any resulting interstices are filled with grout. This method results in a "colder" work and the artists must use their skill and creativeness in order to adjust and touch up the work, even by hammering a board against the mortar when this is not yet completely dry, but still soft.

A combination of the two described techniques is the reciprocal or double reverse method (mosaico a rivoltura).

The process consists in first preparing a shallow bed of sand framed in strips of wood. Then the design is outlined on the sand and the tesserae are set in one by one as in the direct method. Further an adhesive as flour paste or another soluble one is applied on the tesserae and several layers of gauze are spread on top and allowed to dry on. The frame is then turned upside down and the strips of wood, sand or lime removed so that the top parts of the tesserae appear and the mosaic can be applied to its permanent support.

The mosaico a rivoltura results in a flat, smooth surface of the work which quite lacks the sense of movements obtained when the tesserae are directly inserted one by one. Needless to say the direct method consists of a longer and more expensive process.

97
MUNITION
OF
VITREOUS
PASTES
*at the
Orsoni glass
factory,
Venice*

*Sightseeing
and other
relevant
openings*

"PIETRE DURE"

A related art to mosaic is that of "commesso" or pietre dure(literally hard stones). It can be regarded as a type of "mosaic" of stones such as lapis lazuli, jasper, porphyry, chalcedony and others *arranged in decorative patterns* and inlaid in wooden panels and plaques.

From the Opificio delle Pietre Dure in Florence set up around 1572 with Milanese and local craftsmen, the panels were shipped all over Europe and used by cabinet-makers and for table-tops.

As to the origin of the art, Prof. Gonzales-Palacios traces it with no doubt in Rome, in contrast with other scholars who ascribe the origin to other centres, as examples of pietre dure have been found in the Northern regions of Italy, mainly in Milano and Genova areas as early as 1500.

It was however in Florence that much interest in the art of pietre dure arose under the Medici family, who were instrumental in the setting of the Opificio which was active until the late 1870's.

It is of course in this city that one can admire marvelous works in the Museo dell'Opificio delle Pietre Dure, in the Museo degli Argenti, in the Palazzo Pitti, in the Church of San Lorenzo etc. Many other examples are scattered to an extent virtually everywhere, e.g. V&A Museum, London, Allen Art Museum in Oberlin, Ohio, El Prado Museum, Madrid, etc. and *99* in *private collections in Italy* and abroad.

Italian craftsmen were also called to work in Prague and Madrid, where the manufactures were under the sponsorship of Emperor Rudolf II and Charles III respectively.

Prof. F. Rossi also advances the hypothesis, supported by other writers, that the Florentine craft of pietra dura even influenced the intarsio *100* work of palaces at Delhi and *Agra*, as the presence of Tuscan masters has been documented at the Court of the Grand Moghul around 1648.

N.B. For those readers who would like to enlarge upon the subject of "Pietre Dure", a rich bibliographical list is given in the issue no. 20 of "I Nuovi Quaderni dell'Antiquariato" (Gonzales-Palacios, Fabbri Editore).

THE "COSMATIS AND VASSALLETTOS"

The Cosmatis are a family of "marmorai romani" that were very active in many cities of central Italy in the XIII and XIV centuries. Marmorai means "stonecutters", but this generic popular name includes also mosaicists, sculptors, architects.

The denomination Cosmati most probably derives from the name Cosma, so frequently used among the artists who devoted themselves to the peculiar art of the "intarsio" known as "cosmatesque". This consists in the use of large marble tesserae (predominantly in the green and red colour) to decorate large marble surfaces. These are *seen on church floors*, amboni, pulpits, episcopal chairs, candelabra, baptisimal fonts etc. Often in the decoration are added the more expensive gold vitreous tesserae.

The inspiration of the Cosmatis' work is in prevalence classical and can be compared to the Roman "opus sectile".

Several churches in Rome offer examples of Cosmatesque art.

Contemporary of the Cosmatis were also another family of marmorai, the Vassallettos. Their work is quite similar to the Cosmatis' and can be seen at its best in the cloister of S. Giovanni in Laterano and St. Paul's-outside-the Wall in Rome.

100
FLORAL PATTERN
IN PIETRA DURA
AGRA, INDIA

101
S. SEBASTIAN
(VII cent.)
Byzantine iconography
of this famous saint
that has inspired so
many artists!
CHURCH
OF S. PETER AD
VINCULA, ROME

FIVE ITINERARIES TO DISCOVER THE MOSAICS
OF THE ETERNAL CITY

The choice of the following itineraries has been made because of the relative ease with which they may be made on foot.

First itinerary: ST.PETERS'BASILICA AND VATICAN MUSEUMS

A1   *At the entrance* of the Basilica, above the main gate opposite the Filarete Door, is *La Navicella* work of Giotto. Almost completely remade in the XVI century. Inside the church view all the altar-pieces, central and lateral cupolas (read the Chapter on the Studio del Mosaico Vaticano). An inscription runs all round the drum of the cupola, the apse and along the central nave and transept, magnificent example of mosaic epigraphy. In the confession, under Bernini's baldacchino, in the Pallii Niche, see *Mosaic of the Saviour* (IX century)

A2   *Vatican Grottoes*, fragments of ancient mosaics from the demolished church. In the Scavi (necropo lis) the Mausoleum of the Julii, mosaic of *Christ as "Helios" the Sun, driving his chariot*. It is considered the oldest extant Christian subject, dated III/IV century.

A3   *In the Vatican Museum*: Mosaics exhibited at the entrance. Theater Masks in the Gabinetto delle Maschere, Landscape from Hadrian's Villa. Room of the Animals: two emblemata with animal scenes and two mosaic floors
Sala Rotonda (Round Hall) floor mosaic from Otricoli, nr. Rome with sea-divinities and battle with the centaurs.

102 CHRIST AS HELIOS (II/III cent.)
Considered to be the earliest image of Christ.
MAUSOLEUM OF THE JULII, GROTTE VATICANE, ST. PETERS'
VATICAN CITY

Sala a Croce Greca (Greek-Cross Room) Mosaic floor with Minerva and the moon phases.

Museo Pio-Cristiano (Christian Museum) Head of an Apostle from the Lateran Triclinium plus other classical mosaics in the nearby room on the left.

Museo Gregoriano: asaraton floor (unswept) from the Aventine villa.

N.B. *Close observation during the visit will reveal other mosaics.*

Second itinerary   AREA OF ESQUILINE

B1   ***Church of St Peter in Chains*** – *Mosaic of St.Sebastian* (VII century) Byzantine iconography more realist than the one presented during the Renaissance that depicts the saint as Adonis. St. Sebastian is the protector against pestilence and epidemics. This basilica is much visited, because it houses the statue of Moses by Michelangelo.   *101*

B2   ***Basilica of St.Prassede*** – Mosaics of the IX century of the so-called Carolingian Renaissance (Charlemagne's attempt to revive the fastii of imperial Rome) and Mosaics of the chapel of S.Zenone (right nave)

B3   ***Basilica of Santa Pudenziana*** – IV century mosaic – in the apse: Seated figure of Christ, flanked by Apostles and perhaps the two sisters SS. Pudenziana and Prassede. A noteworthy appropriation in a Christian context of the language and form of the classical art

B4   ***Basilica St. Mary Major*** – Along the central nave and on the triumphal arch V century mosaics with stories of the Old Testament and scenes of the Childhood of Jesus
In the Apse, *Coronation of the Virgin,* the master-   *54*

piece of the Franciscan mosaicist Jacopo Turriti (XIII century)
Exterior facade, partly covered by the loggia, XIII century mosaics by Filippo Rusuti

Third Itinerary: FROM THE COLOSSEUM TO ST. JOHN LATERAN

C1   ***Church of S.Clemente***
A two-level church, built on remains of a Roman House and a Mithraeum. XII century mosaic in the apse showing the Triumph of the Cross. This is the great symbol of *the Cross-Arbor Vitae* stemming from the leaves of the acanthus bush. A myriad of plants, animals, birds, fish and human figures are hidden in the scrolled leaves.

103

C2   ***Baptistry of St.John Lateran***
Various mosaics dated V-VII centuries

C3   ***Basilica of St. John Lateran***
Apsidal mosaics by Jacopo Turriti, (XIII century) but completely restored in the XIX century.
Lateran Triclinium – Apse with mosaics of the VIII century but restored in the XVIII century, showing the two great Christian Emperors, Constantine and Charlemagne
Sancta Sanctorum, the medieval papal chapel before the popes' transfer to the Vatican.
Mosaics done either by Giotto or Pietro Cavallini in the XIII century.

Fourth Itinerary: TRASTEVERE AREA

D1   ***Church of S. Crysogone*** – Mosaics below the semi-dome and panel of Madonna with the SS.Crysogone and James

132

D2   *Church of St. Maria in Trastevere*
XII century mosaics of the facade and XIII century
mosaics of the Apse plus those already mentioned
by *Pietro Cavallini* (two panels with stories of the   53
Virgin)

D3   *Basilica S. Cecilia* XII century mosaics in the apse
with Christ and Saints on a background of red end
purple clouds.

Fifth Itinerary: CENTRAL AREA

E1   *Palazzo Altemps* (near Piazza Navona)
Mosaic from an imperial villa at Castel Porziano near
Rome, with hunting scenes, combats, sea scenes etc.
(II century)

E2   *Museo Napoleonico and Museo Praz*
Pay a visit here if you wish to form an idea of the
"mosaico minuto" (XVIII and XIX centuries)

E3   *Piazza Augusto Imperatore* – XX century
mosaics on the top facades of the buildings surrounding the piazza. They date from the Fascist era.

E4   *Church of St.Maria del Popolo*   55
Chigi Chapel, with mosaics by Luigi Pace from cartoons by Raphael. (*Eternal Father, sun and planets,
angels*) (XVI century)

N.B. We also suggest a visit to the Museo Nazionale Romano, near the
Termini Station, to admire beautiful Roman floor mosaics, and to the
Antiquario Comunale.

103
ARBOR-VITAE or
The Triumph of the
Cross (XII cent.)
*A real "triumph" of
colour and designs!
CHURCH
OF S. CLEMENTE,
ROME*

135

GLOSSARY

ACANTHUS
: prickly plant stylised in scroll form

APSE
: a recess of semicircular shape in the wall at the end of a building (normally at the end of the central nave of a church)

CARTOON
: design outlined on cloth or paper for use when normally transferring mosaic onto a wall or vault

CEMENT
: from the Latin "coementum", a kind of concrete made up of mortar and stone. The word is also used in a broader sense to designate various adhesives used to bind together different materials such as mosaic tesserae

COCCIO
: literally "a crock". In certain regions of Italy it indicates a vase or ornamental piece of terracotta

COCCIOPESTO
: crushed potsherds. Formed of two words, "coccio" a piece of terracotta and "pesto" a root from the verb "pestare" or to pound, to mixed with lime and applied directly as a pavement, or as a foundation in which mosaic tesserae were set to make a mosaic pavement

COLLANTE
: a material serving as an adhesive

EMBLEMA
: (plural Emblemata) central panel of a mosaic pavement, normally prepared in a workshop with finer tesserae and set in a terracotta or marble tray and later embedded in the pavement. Usually of high quality

FILATI
: a dense substance, including glass, melted and drawn into threads

FORNACIARO
: glass-maker

GROUT
: liquid mortar poured to fill the interstices between the tesserae

GUILLOCHE
: linear pattern composed of two or more mul-

	ticoloured strands or several braided strands. It originated in textiles.
GUM MASTIC	mixture of various substances employed to fix the tesserae of a mosaic on a support
LITHOSTROTON	a floor made of stones
MEANDER	also Fret or Greek Key – continuous swastikas to form a pattern of a mosaic
MORTAR	mixture of cement, lime, sand and water used to hold together tesserae
OPUS	literally "work"
OPUS VERMICULATUM	worm-like opus. Mosaic created with sinuous lines imitating wall painting
REPERTORY	pattern book – collection of designs, patterns of motifs used by mosaicists
SINOPIA	Name derived from the city of Sinope in Asia Minor famous for its red pigment used in the preparation of the drawing and underpainting on which to imbed the tesserae of a mosaic or paint the colours of a fresco.
SMALTO	molten glass, the base for tesserae
SPOLVERO	technique to transfer the cartoon on the surface to be painted or covered with mosaic. It consists of pricking small holes along the outlines of the drawing and then dust them with charcoal powder, so that small dots result on the plaster, as a reference for the painter.
STACCO	technique to detach (staccare) from their original places, both mosaics and frescoes.
TESSERAE	fragments of marble, stone, terracotta, glass or other materials which are used to make up mosaics. Generally cubic in form, their size varies within the range of a few centimetres
TRICLINIUM	dining-room in the Roman house where guests were entertained
VITRARIUS	glass-maker
VITREOUS PASTE	material made of fused glass from which mosaic tesserae can be obtained

SELECTED BIBLIOGRAPHY

Literature on mosaic is very broad. Unfortunately many of the books are quite expensive or out-of-print. They can though be found on the shelves of major libraries. Just to mention the New York Public Library, they have got 68 entries on the subject of mosaics. Of course many of the books are academic publications, but it is up to the reader to look for what he/she needs.

We believe that the following list will help the reader to enlarge upon the themes treated in the present book.

A Handbook of Roman Art edited by Martin Henig – Phaidon Press, 1983

Alfieri, Branchetti, Cornini, *Mosaici Minuti Romani del 700 e dell'800*, Edizioni del Mosaico 1986

S. Aurigemma, *The mosaics of Tripolitania*, Tome I of "Italy in Africa"

C. Bertelli, *Il mosaico*, Mondadori Editore

J.R. Clarke, *Roman black and white figural mosaics*, New York University Press, 1979

J. Mellentin Haswell, *Mosaic*, Thames and Hudson 1973

R. Ling, *Ancient Mosaics*, Princeton University Press 1998

Gonzales-Palacios, *The art of Mosaics*, Selections from the Gilbert Collection, L.A. County Museum of Art, 1977

D. Petochi, I.F. Roncuzzi, *Tecnologia del mosaico*, Ed. Longo, Ravenna

F. Rossi, *Mosaic*, Alfieri Lacroix 1989 (with a large section dedicated to Pietra Dura

S. Röttgen, *Roman Mosaics from the XVI to XIX century*, 1982

R. Talbot-Rice, *Byzantine Art*, Thames & Hudson

LIST OF SPECIAL PICTURES

Front and back covers

DIONYSUS WATERING FLOWERS (II cent.)
Bacchus to the Romans. He is the god of wine and revelry.
He symbolizes not only the intoxicating power of wine but also its social and
beneficent influence, therefore the god is viewed as promoter of civilization.
UPPER GANGWAY, VATICAN MUSEUM, VATICAN CITY

MANDOLIN PLAYER (Mid. XIX cent. micromosaic)
Broach mounted on silver. Typical object bought by some Grand tourist at a
Spanish Steps' workshop. PRIVATE COLLECTION

1 (page 2) - APOLLO CYTHARAEDUS (Roman copy of a Greek original)
Patron of the arts and inventor of music. Also said to be the first physician.
SALA DELLE MUSE, VATICAN MUSEUM, VATICAN CITY

3 (page 9) - ANGEL (IX cent.)
Detail of apsidal mosaic CHURCH OF SANTA SOPHIA, SALONIKA, GREECE

27 (pag. 40) - CHRIST (IV cent. A.D.)
Standing in the center of the apse on clouds rendered in bold colours. He is
flanked (not seen in this picture) by the two brothers
Cosmas and Damian, famous healers and patron saints of physicians.
CHURCH OF SS. COSMAS AND DAMIAN, ROME

49 (pag. 62) - TITIAN CONTROLS THE WORKS ON ST. MARK'S
CATHEDRAL IN COMPANY OF MOSAICIST A. ZUCCATO (XIX cent.)
Detail on the facade of Palazzo Barbarigo on the Grand Canal, she of the
Compagnia Venezia-Murano, VENICE

50 (pag. 63) - NATIVITY SCENE (XIX cent.)
Cartoon provided by Van Neef of the School opened by Csar Nicholas I
CHURCH OF ST. ISAAC, ST. PETERSBURG

62 (pag. 78) - GEORGE IV, KING OF ENGLAND (XIX cent.)
This is a mosaic copy after the original painting by Thomas Lawrence housed in
the Vatican Museum
THE ROYAL PAVILLION ART GALLERY AND MUSEUM, BRIGHTON, ENGLAND

77 (pag. 92) - VESTAL (XIX cent.)
by the mosaicist Clemente Ciuli active in Rome in the first half of XIX century.
He is remembered as one the best artists in the micromosaic technique.
MUSÉE DU JARDIN DES PLANTES, PARIS

78 (pag. 93)VIEW OF THE ROMAN FORUM (Early XIX cent.)
Micromosaic broach mounted on gold. PRIVATE COLLECTION

84 (pag. 104) - PERSIAN SYBIL (XVIII cent.)
Perhaps after the cartoon of Guido Reni. Executed in Rome by the mosaicist
Mattia Moretti. Gift presented by the Corsini Family to the Granduke of Tuscany
Leopold. - *GALLERIA DEGLI UFFIZI, FLORENCE*

99 (pag. 125) - SUNFLOWER (XVII cent.)
Pietre dure panl, after J. Ligozzi
MUSEO DELL'OPIFICIO PIETRE DURE, FLORENCE

PHOTOGRAPHIC ACKNOWLEDGEMENTS

Archivi Alinari, Florence: 2, 11, 17, 18, 38, 45, 46, 47, 101 - Trustees of the British Museum, London: 7, 25 - Foto Elio e Stefano Ciol, Casarsa, Italy: 34, 50, 76, 91, 97 - Fabbri , Milan: 64, 65 - Foto Gioberti, Rome: 72, 78, 88, 89, 90, *back cover* - Leeds Museums and Galleries (City Musem), Leeds: 21 - Silvana Mazzoni: Rome: 41, 42, 43 - Musée Archeologique de Saint Romain en Gal, Vienne, France: 22 - Foto Musei Vaticani, Vatican City: 1, 12, 14, 20, 85, *front cover* - Servizio Fotografico de "L'Osservatore Romano", Vatican City: 83 - Ag. Laura Ronchi, Milan: 49, 73 - R.C.S. Libri Spa, Milan: 67, 77 (Baguzzi) 86 (Permission of F. Patridge) - Archivio Scala, Florence: 9, 10, 15, 23, 24, 28, 30, 31, 32, 33, 39, 48, 51, 52, 53, 54, 55, 56, 57, 58, 59, 60, 61, 63, 82, 84, 102, 103 - By permission of Don Enzo Buschi, Cathedral of Macerata, Italy: 79 - By permission of Father Nicola, Minotenkirche, Vienna: 87 - By permission of the Royal Pavillion Art Gallery and Museum, Brighton: 62 - By permission of the United Nations Library, N.Y.: 75 - By the Author: 71

N.B.: Regretfully for some photos it has not been possible to track down any source. The author will be pleased to mention them should they become available in the future.

75 THE GOLDEN RULE (XX cent.)
"Do unto others as you would have them do unto you"
NORMAN ROCKWELL, U.N. HEADQUARTERS, NEW YORK CITY, U.S.A.

*Roman by birth the author took her licence as a
professional guide in 1971. Since then she has
been conducting tours of the Eternal City and its
surroundings in Italian, English and French.
She also conducts regular visits of the Vatican
Museums and Gardens.
The inspiration to write this book came to her
at the suggestion of her many customers wanting
to learn more on the art of mosaic without burdening
themselves with too in depth academic publications.
She hopes of having filled a gap and her wish is that
the book will prove an enjoyable reading
for everyone.*